SUNRISE

*A SUPPORT GROUP PROGRAM FOR
CHILDREN OF DIVORCED PARENTS*

by

Virginia McCall, PBVM

PAULIST PRESS

New York and Mahwah, N.J.

The Publisher gratefully acknowledges permission to use material from: *The Children's Beginning Experience Manual* edited by Cecelia Bennett (Beginning Experience Central Office, 302 Michigan Ave., Detroit, MI 48206, 1980) which appears on pages 19, 20, 47.

Library of Congress Cataloging-in-Publication Data

McCall, Virginia, 1935–
    Sunrise : a support group program for children of divorced parents / by Virginia McCall
      p.   cm.
    ISBN 0-8091-3330-X (pbk.) :
    1. Children of divorced parents--Counseling of.   2. Group counseling of children.
  3. Divorce--Problems, exercises, etc.
  I. Title.
  HQ777.5M38   1992
  306.89–dc20
                                    92-26329
                                       CIP

Published by Paulist Press
997 Macarthur Boulevard
Mahwah, New Jersey 07430

Printed and bound in the United States of America

CONTENTS

ACKNOWLEDGEMENTS

I wish to thank everyone who has contributed in any way to the development of SUNRISE and completion of the SUNRISE program.

Janet Gendusa, Rebecca Fein and Jean Messina who worked to pilot this program, contributed to its development and participated in training leaders for SUNRISE in the Archdiocese of Miami.

Deb Nelson, PBVM, Janice Klein, PBVM, Colette Baldwin, RSM, Maureen Duffy, Father Robert Bozek, Cecelia Bennett, Elaine Syfert, Carol Boyle and Robert Farmer, Ph.D. for their input, professional advice and expertise.

Maria Jetton whose computer skills prepared the manuscript for publication.

Carol Farrell and Maureen Duffy for their constant encouragement to create and to prepare the SUNRISE program for publication.

I would like to acknowledge that material found on pp. 19, 20 and 47 is from the *Children's Beginning Experience Manual*.

PREFACE

SUNRISE is a peer support group for children of any age whose parents are divorced. The group is under the direction of an adult trained to work with children who are dealing with loss.

This manual is divided into seven sections, each containing material which can be used at any time throughout the SUNRISE sessions. Read through the entire manual before using it with the children so that you will be acquainted with how everything is interconnected. There are some activities used during the early sessions which are further developed at a later time. Return to specific topics as particular feelings and/or issues arise in the group.

Preceding each section are introductory remarks and background information for the leader, followed by reproducible activities which can be used to help children come in touch with their experience and to initiate sharing. Specific ages are not indicated on the activities. Rather than categorize them into particular age levels, it is left to the leader to determine what is most appropriate for the group and to make the necessary adaptations.

SUNRISE is a flexible program which can be adapted to the needs of the group. It has sufficient material to be a program in itself. However, group leaders are encouraged to develop other exercises and experiences appropriate to the age level and the needs of a particular group.

Ideally, SUNRISE runs parallel to a group program for parents. If this is not possible, it is important to have a meeting with parents at the beginning of the SUNRISE program. At this time they can be informed about what will be covered in the program and encouraged to respect the privacy of their children who may not be willing to share with them what they do or say in their SUNRISE group.

INTRODUCTION

Children become the innocent victims when their parents divorce. Part of this is the consequence of their own loss. However, it is often further complicated by the inability of one or both parents, absorbed by their feelings and issues, to be emotionally and sometimes physically available to their children. During this time it is essential that children have some adult— teacher, relative, friend, counselor—in whom they can confide and who can serve as a role model for them.

SUNRISE has been developed to offer children the opportunity to deal with their loss as a result of their parents' divorce. Because it is a peer support group, it also helps children realize that they are not alone in their experience.

Studies have been done to determine what age is most greatly affected by the divorce of parents. Actually the life of every child is significantly touched by the loss of a parent. However, for the most part, to the degree that the custodial parent recovers from his or her experience of divorce and is able to continue on with life in a healthy and positive way, so will the children. This process takes time. It can take years.

SUNRISE is not therapy. It is not for children with severe emotional difficulties or who are extremely traumatized by their parents' divorce. These children need to be referred for professional counseling.

Rather, SUNRISE is for those children who need some basic information and are willing to join with other children to talk about their loss as a way of dealing with their pain and confusion. It requires a willingness on their part not only to share their feelings and their struggle but to offer encouragement and support to others in the group. It is a commitment on their part to attend the sessions and to participate as fully as possible.

According to Judith Wallerstein, children move through six significant developmental tasks as they recover from the effects of their parents' divorce.[1]

Task I:
Acknowledging the Reality of the Marital Rupture

Children move through a grieving process the same as adults—denial, anger, bargaining, depression, and acceptance. Before the recovery process can even begin, children must move beyond the denial of their parents' separation and divorce and admit the reality.

One child told her friend that her father was on a business trip. The friend shared her confusion with her mother: "Mom, Mary says her dad is on a business trip and will be back home soon. I know her parents are getting a divorce and that's why he's gone. She's lying to me."

Her friend really was not lying. She needed so badly to deny the reality of her parents' divorce that she really believed the story she was telling.

Task II:
Disengaging from Parental Conflict and Distress and Resuming Customary Pursuits

Children are often caught in the middle of their parents' angry outbursts as well as battles over custody and settlement issues. They easily become the vehicle through which parents get even with one another.

In an effort to deny their reality there is a tendency for one or both parents to run from the pain. This can be done by constant busyness, alcohol, drugs, involvement in a new rela-

---

1. Judith S. Wallerstein, "Children of Divorce: The Psychological Tasks of the Child," *American Journal of Orthopsychiatry*, 1983, pp. 230-243.

tionship, sexual acting out, or anything which becomes a compulsive way to negate the pain and leave one feeling momentarily worthwhile and loved. Such running, especially by the custodial parent, can leave children without the physical presence of a parent during a time it is needed so badly.

Divorcing persons are usually overwhelmed by a complexity of feelings—anger, guilt, depression, loneliness, bitterness, fear, alienation from friends, rejection and a sense of failure and low self-esteem. As they deal with these feelings, it is often difficult, if not impossible, for them to be emotionally present to their children.

Rather than being constantly absorbed in their parents' conflict and grieving process and feeling responsible to take care of their parents, children need to be encouraged to maintain their usual activities and relationships.

Task III:
Resolution of the Loss

This task takes time—years. A child whose parents divorce obviously loses the presence of one parent and experiences the disruption of family life as it has always been. These are further complicated by other significant losses often overlooked or unacknowledged.

Concomitant with divorce is usually a loss of income. There might not be enough money for the food, clothing, entertainment and the overall life style to which the child was accustomed. The divorce may require a move from a familiar home, neighborhood and school. Friends and teachers who offered some sense of continuity and security are no longer present.

Each significant loss must be grieved by the child. However, children, too, have a tendency to run from their pain. They may become lost in a world of activity and/or fantasy. It is not unusual for a child to regress back to a time when he or she felt safe and secure. A six year old stated to his mother, "I wish I could go back in a time machine. Then you and Daddy would be here to take care of me." This same child had actually regressed to bed-wetting and baby-talk,

behavior of a time in his life when he had felt safe and secure.

Children may move to the other extreme, becoming over-responsible for parent(s) and siblings. They may become the bully, the clown or the model student in an effort to hide the crying inside, for their pain can be overwhelming.

They, too, deal with the same kinds of feelings as their parents—fear, anger, guilt, abandonment, insecurity, loneliness, shame, helplessness and confusion. They may feel unloved, isolated and helpless to do anything about the situation. Often they are embarrassed because they feel they alone have parents who are divorced, and they attempt to hide this reality from others. They worry about their parents and about their own future. Even as they deal with their own pain, they are confronted with the emotional distress of their parent(s).

Children need some way to acknowledge and to deal positively with their feelings of loss. This can be done through professional counseling, sharing with a trusted friend or adult or within a peer support group.

Task IV:
Resolving Anger and Self-Blame

Because their world revolves around themselves, children tend to feel responsible for the breakdown of the marriage. They reason that it must be because of something they did or didn't do or say. Children need to be led to understand that divorce is an adult problem over which they have no control.

Resolving anger can be a tedious process. Like adults, children can project their anger in many directions. Angry because their father or mother is gone, children might express hostility toward that absent person. However, if they feel secure with their custodial parent, this may be where their anger is directed. They know this parent won't leave them.

Teachers and peers can also be the target of a child's anger as they attempt to express their confusion, their feeling of isolation, and their need to be heard.

Seven year old Billy's behavior was becoming unmanageable in school. When asked what he was feeling, he replied. "I feel like I'm invisible. I try to tell 'em how much I hurt, but they don't listen. So I punch 'em good!"

Children need to identify and to talk about their anger so they can learn healthy and positive ways of dealing with it.

Task V:
Accepting the Permanence of the Divorce

Children might be able to acknowledge their parents' divorce, but it takes much longer to realize that this is a permanent reality. This is closely related to the previous task of dealing with self-blame. If children think they have the power to separate their parents, then certainly they must also be able to reunite them.

Children can become totally preoccupied with plans for bringing their parents together again. Part of their recovery is to realize that they have no control over the situation. Dad and Mom are not going to live together again—ever.

Task VI:
Achieving Realistic Hope
Regarding Relationships

It is really difficult to trust again after feeling abandoned by one parent and perhaps not trusting either one. This task is one which can take many years to resolve.

A child needs to discover a balance between two extremes. On the one hand, there might be a tendency to become overly dependent on a person of the opposite sex and to compulsively seek relationships which appear to provide security. On the other hand, a young person can reject any relationship with the opposite sex out of fear of being abandoned again.

Children need to grow in their experience of trusting their peers. They need adult role models from whom they can learn that others are worthy of their trust. Children need to be led to a greater understanding of the positive aspects of marriage and commitment. They need to develop skills in communication and for dealing with conflict in a healthy manner.

JOURNALING

Journaling can be done by children twelve years old and older. It is a means by which they can reflect upon their experience in a way that can be healing and at the same time private.

Encourage older children to obtain a notebook which they can decorate in any way they wish. The journal is like a diary in which they write their thoughts and feelings each day. It can serve as a means of helping them to sort out their reaction to their parents' divorce and to make some choices to move on with their life. They can express themselves through whatever medium appeals to them: art, poetry, stories, dialogue, etc.

When using the journal, suggest that they find a quiet place where they can be alone. It is helpful for them to be relaxed before writing. This can be done by having them take a few minutes to sit quietly with eyes closed. Ask them to breathe in deeply through their nose, hold their breath briefly and exhale through their mouth.

Once they feel peaceful and relaxed, they can either begin writing whatever thoughts, feelings, and experiences related to their parents divorce come to mind or they can use the "Journal Writing" handout found at the end of each section.

Some children may hesitate to express their true thoughts and feelings in their journal out of fear that what they've written will fall into the hands of others. Talk to them about how this privacy can be maintained.

The handouts can also be used as part of the group session. However, children should be allowed to share only what they feel comfortable sharing within the group. What they write in their journal is private material.

LET'S BEGIN

- To begin developing feelings of comfort and trust
- To determine the purpose of the group
- To establish ground rules
- To determine personal goals and commitment

When children first come together to form a SUNRISE group, they often feel awkward and embarrassed. Therefore the first task of the leader is to help them feel at ease and to lay some groundwork for sharing their feelings and the experience of their parents' divorce.

As with everything presented in this manual, the leader may wish to return to these activities to deepen relationships or to break the tension.

There will be many opportunities for children to process their experience through drawing and writing. Each child will need a folder or a large paper bag in which to place these activities. In this way they can save whatever they wish. One of the first suggested activities is to design this folder or bag so children can easily identify their materials. To respect their privacy, no names are used on any of the activities. Children might want to develop their own picture-code to place on their belongings. Emphasize the need for privacy and that their projects are safe with you. It is essential that you honor this trust.

Children might equate the use of too many handouts with school work. It will be up to you to vary the type of activities used. Whenever possible, use the handout for your information as a means of further exploration and in-depth sharing. Use your own creativity to adapt the following material to the style and medium most appropriate to your group of children.

Getting To Know You: The following "Getting To Know You" activities are suggested ways through which the children can become better acquainted. The length of time spent on these activities will vary. Children who have a previous relationship with one another will not require as long as those who come together as total strangers. Some will need several sessions just developing a sense of trust before they will feel free enough to talk about their experience and their feelings of loss. Be patient and give them whatever time they need.

Purpose: Some children might be in the SUNRISE group because one of their parents told them they had to come. They might be defensive and hostile. Others might be present because they have specific issues they want to talk about. Some are just curious.

Whatever their reason for being part of the group, it helps children to verbalize them. When they hear the responses from one another, they begin to form a better understanding of what the group is all about and that others have similar experiences, questions and feelings.

As the leader of this group, you may wish to elicit responses from the children, placing them on a chalk board or poster paper. However, you may find the activities under "Purpose" to be helpful in formulating what can be accomplished through the SUNRISE group.

As you guide the children in expressing their reasons for being in SUNRISE, be aware of the following overall purpose of the program:

- To bring children together whose parents are divorced
- To talk about similar experiences, feelings and concerns

- To offer support to one another in a peer group
- To gain a better understanding of what is happening in their lives
- To learn some skills to help cope with their situation

Remember that this is not a therapy group. Rather, you are present to walk with the children as they talk about their experience and their pain. Your role is to provide a safe atmosphere and the opportunity to deal with their loss in a constructive, positive way.

Guidelines: SUNRISE is a group to which children are invited. If they do not want to be there, don't pressure them. Otherwise they can create behavior problems which will be destructive to the progress of the entire group.

At the same time, realize that the children in your SUNRISE group are dealing with the normal difficulties related to their ages plus the trauma of adjusting to so many changes. Therefore, in spite of their desire to be in the group, there will be times when children will act out their anger and their confusion about what is happening in their lives.

For this reason there is a need for some specific ground rules. Keep these rules simple and as fair as possible. Have the children talk about what guidelines will be necessary for their group. You or one of the children can make a poster with these guidelines which can be displayed at each meeting. How this is done and the depth of the ground rules will of course depend upon the maturity of the children.

As you develop these guidelines, it is essential to include confidentiality and listening. Talk about the importance of keeping within the group what is shared by other children. With younger children you might need to tell them that there are certain things that are private within families, and that if they begin to move into this area, you will suggest to them that they can talk to you alone about that particular issue.

Confidentiality also protects the children. They need to know that they can share what they've said in the group with their parent(s) only if they want to do so. They need to be able to trust you. Let them know that in most cases you will hold in confidence what each child shares. However, children need to be told that in situations in which they could be hurt, you will need to contact the appropriate persons but you will not do this without first informing the particular child involved.

Listening is extremely important but so difficult, especially for the young children. Help them to understand that each child is important and has a right to be heard. Listening to one another can help them to discover new ways to cope with a particular situation. Listening to one another also shows that each child is respected and valued.

You may wish to develop a method to deal with behavior problems within the group. If the sharing becomes too heavy for the child to handle, he or she can be given the option of moving to another part of the room to work alone quietly. Materials can be made available so that the child can use this time to write or to draw what he or she is feeling. Or there can be some books available to read. If the group is in a school setting, the child can return to the classroom. If this is an out-of-school program, it is helpful to have someone available to take a child into another room. However, sometimes the child just needs some physical distance, but be close enough to hear what is being said by others.

Remind the children that they have a choice of behaving appropriately. If they choose to misbehave, they automatically leave the group. You can say something like, "I'm sorry you choose not to be with us today. I hope to see you next week."

Often when children feel uncomfortable, they express this through laughter. It will help to talk about this. Remind them that everyone deserves respect. There are times when one of them will express their pain, and this can trigger feelings in others. Rather than cover up their uncomfortableness by laughing, encourage them to attempt to honestly express what they are feeling. As the group leader, you can help the child who laughs to explore his or her feelings rather than correct him or her for inappropriate behavior.

Make the environment in which your group meets as comfortable and pleasant as possible. If the room is large enough, children can bring pillows and sit on the floor. They can take off their shoes. If appropriate, provide some juice and crackers for them to have either during their sharing or afterward.

Goals: This section includes activities for goal-setting so that the children will have some idea of where they are going and a sense of accomplishment when they leave SUNRISE.

The activities under "Goals" can be used not only to establish goals but as a means of communicating to the children some changes in their thinking and in their behavior which can positively affect future relationships.

Place emphasis upon *their* thinking and behavior because they are the only ones they can change. Their hope will always be that they can change their parents or that they can bring their parents together again. This is not realistic but they often become absorbed and preoccupied by thoughts of how to bring this about. Help them to be realistic in setting their goals.

There is also an activity at the end of the SUNRISE program in which the children look back at these original goals to see what they have actually achieved.

Commitment: Following this section you will find a contract. This is only to be used in specific situations. If a child does not want to attend the group, but a parent thinks it will be helpful, use the contract. Sit down with the child and ask him or her to give the group a chance. The contract can be used as a way of establishing an agreement to participate for a certain number of sessions. After that time, if the child chooses to leave the group, it is all right.

The contract can also be a commitment on the part of the parent to set SUNRISE as a priority for their children.

LET'S PRETEND

MATERIALS NEEDED: Optional: *LET'S PRETEND* handout

PURPOSE: To provide an enjoyable, non-threatening way for younger children to get acquainted and to begin the process of trusting one another.

DIRECTIONS: Have the children sit in a circle and say to them:

It's fun to make believe. Let's pretend we can go anywhere and be anything we want.

I'll begin and you follow what I say. After we've gone around the circle a couple times someone else can be the leader.

My name is _____.

If I could be an animal, I would be a _____

because _____.

My name is _____.

If I could fly, I would _____

because _____

My name is _____.

If I could go anywhere, I would go to _____

because _____.

Children can take turns leading with similar phrases.

Younger children can color the animals or draw a picture of the animal they'd like to be and tell why they chose that particular animal.

LET'S PRETEND

MY FAVORITE THINGS

MATERIALS NEEDED: Depending on the approach used: pencils, crayons, magic markers or colored pencils, paper, magazine pictures, scissors, glue, clay, *MY FAVORITE THINGS* handout, paper bag or drawing paper

PURPOSE: To provide the opportunity for children to think about some of the more positive things in their life.

Following the activity children share their "favorites" with one another. This is an enjoyable and non-threatening way for them to begin sharing something about themselves.

DIRECTIONS: • Using *MY FAVORITE THINGS* handout:

Young children can color these pictures and then tell the group their favorite food, color, etc. — always prefacing their response with "My name is _____."

• Using a Paper Bag or Free Drawing:

Have children draw their "favorites" on a large paper bag and color them.

• Making a Collage:

Have available a variety of pictures. Give each child scissors, glue and paper. Ask them to choose five or six (depending on the number of available pictures) pictures which they like. Glue them to the paper. Tell them that you will be asking them to share with the group why they made the choices they did.

• Using Clay:

Give each child some clay and ask them to make a model of their favorite animal, sport, etc. They can then show their creation to the group and talk about it.

MY FAVORITE THINGS!

MY FAVORITES

MATERIALS NEEDED: *MY FAVORITES* handout, pencil

PURPOSE: This is a way for older children to share who they are in a non-threatening manner. It also moves them a bit deeper by asking them to look at the effect of their choices and their actions on others.

DIRECTIONS: Give each child *MY FAVORITES* handout. Ask them to list their "favorites" under each heading. Refer to the directions at the bottom and remind them to indicate how their choices affect others. Give them some examples such as: Loud music might upset a parent. Favorite places might be something the family can do together. A "favorite" which takes them away from home all the time might interfere with their growth as a family.

When this has been completed, call the group together for sharing. Pay special attention to the effect of their choices on others. Encourage discussion on these. Have them look at the choices with negative effects on others and explore ways that these can be changed.

MY FAVORITES

My Favorite TV Shows

_____

_____

My Favorite Foods

_____

_____

My Favorite Books or Stories

_____

_____

My Favorite Songs

_____

_____

My Favorite Movies

_____

_____

My Favorite Places

_____

_____

In the space below list those "favorites" which have either a positive or a negative effect on others. Next to each indicate what this effect is — especially on members of your family. (Your choice of music might cause your parent or other family members to be upset with you. Your favorite places might be ones where the whole family can go together.)

_____

_____

_____

_____

_____

_____

_____

SELF-PORTRAIT

MATERIALS NEEDED: Drawing paper or *SELF-PORTRAIT* handout, pencils, colored pencils, crayons or magic markers

PURPOSE: To indicate how a child sees himself or herself or how he or she would like to appear. This exercise becomes a way of displaying inner feelings and perhaps relationships if the child includes these in the picture.

At the end of the SUNRISE sessions children are encouraged to again draw a self-portrait in the exercise "How I Have Changed" in Section VI. In this way they can compare the two images of themselves and see the changes that have taken place.

DIRECTIONS: Give each child a piece of drawing paper or the *SELF-PORTRAIT* handout and provide the necessary art supplies.

Draw a picture of yourself. When you have finished write on the paper words which describe you, such as friendly, angry, tough guy, pretty, afraid, etc.

You may want to circulate among the children as they are drawing and ask questions of individuals about what they have drawn and written. This will give you a better understanding of each child.

When the children have completed this project, say to them:

I'm going to collect your pictures and save them until the end of the SUNRISE sessions. Then I'll return them to you. Do not put your name on the paper. You will recognize your own drawing. If you are uncomfortable giving the picture to me, save it in your folder.

SELF-PORTRAIT

GETTING ACQUAINTED

MATERIALS NEEDED: None

PURPOSE: To begin to get acquainted with one another in a way which is fun and non-threatening.

DIRECTIONS: Have the children sit so they make two straight lines facing each other. Each child needs a partner.

Partners introduce themselves and tell their favorite color. Then all members of one row shift to the right, making new pairs. Each one introduces himself or herself and tells how many brothers and sisters he or she has. Continue in this way as long as you wish to gain more information, i.e. where they live (apartment, house, farm), with whom they live, favorite hobby, favorite sport, etc. The questions will depend upon the age of the children.

Then have the children make one large circle. One child says, "My name is _____." Then in turn the others who have exchanged information with that person add to the introduction: "You like the color orange because it reminds you of the sunshine." "You have a little brother who hassles you and a big sister who bosses you." "You live with your dad."

Each child takes his or her turn to be introduced to the group in this way.

WHAT'S ON MY BACK?

MATERIALS NEEDED: Pictures or names of animals, straight pins or tape

PURPOSE: To provide some movement and informal interaction among children as well as the opportunity to become better acquainted.

DIRECTIONS: The leader fastens an animal picture or name on the back of each child. The child's task is to find out what animal is on his or her back. Children may ask "yes" or "no" questions such as: "Would I find this animal on a farm?" "Is it commonly used as a pet?" "Is it large?"

Allow about ten minutes for them to ask the questions. Then they all sit in a circle. The child whose birthday is the closest to January 1 stands and says: "My name is _____.
I think my animal is _____." Someone unfastens what is on the child's back and everyone can see if he or she guessed correctly.

SOME THINGS ABOUT ME

MATERIALS NEEDED: *SOME THINGS ABOUT ME* handout, pencils

PURPOSE: To provide an opportunity for older children to share with one another in a way that can lead to deeper sharing.

To affirm each child and to help all of them understand that it is okay to feel bad or afraid or good. It helps the children to identify their unique qualities and the things they like best about themselves.

DIRECTIONS: Give each child the *SOME THINGS ABOUT ME* handout. Have them find a space in the room where they can answer the questions with some privacy. When they are finished, gather the group together.

Invite the children to share whatever they feel comfortable sharing. Always be aware of their need for privacy and acceptance.

SOME THINGS ABOUT ME

I have _____ brothers and _____ sisters.

I attend _____ School and am in the _____ grade.

My favorite sport is _____

My favorite TV show is _____

My hobbies are _____

Three things I like about myself are:

_____

_____

_____

Some day I hope to _____

I'm afraid of _____ and _____

I am happiest when _____

When I get mad, I _____

My friends like me because _____

_____

Three things that bug me are:

_____

_____

_____

I like people who _____

My best memory is _____

If I had three wishes, I would want _____

_____ and _____

MAKE BELIEVE

MATERIALS NEEDED: Variety of clothing

PURPOSE: It is sometimes easier for children to express themselves when they are dressed differently and pretending to be someone else. This is also fun and adds a bit of variety for long-term groups.

DIRECTIONS: Have each child choose several pieces of clothing which will transform him or her into someone else. Tell them that they will be invited to come forward individually and let their "character" give some words of advice to the group. Or they can talk about how this character is feeling right now.

When the children are ready, bring them together and again give the directions for sharing. You might wish to leave it open-ended so that they can say whatever they wish without giving any guidelines. In this case there will be some who are just silly, but others might share their own feelings and desires.

This is supposed to be just a fun time. However, if anything significant is shared through the "character," allow time to process this with the group before ending the session.

You may want to say something like:

You said that old man is sad and lonely. Do you know anyone who might actually be feeling like this man?

The little child you pretended to be was angry. Do you feel like that child sometimes?

THE ADJECTIVE GAME

MATERIALS NEEDED: Paper 8 1/2 x 11, tape or pins, crayons or magic markers

PURPOSE: To enable children some physical movement at the same time they are getting acquainted. Relating positive adjectives to their name may help a child's sense of self-esteem.

DIRECTIONS:
1. Prepare ahead of time a paper for each child with his or her first name printed on it.

2. Tape or pin the paper on each child's back.

3. Instruct them to mill around the room and introduce themselves to another child.

4. After the introduction, each in turn writes a positive descriptive word under the child's name beginning with the same letter as the name, i.e. CAROL — caring, cheerful.

5. Children then move to another partner, following the same procedure until everyone has met.

6. Remove the paper and allow children time to read the adjectives to the group.

BUILDING BLOCKS

MATERIALS NEEDED: *BUILDING BLOCKS* handout, pencils, crayons or magic markers

PURPOSE: This activity invites children to risk sharing who they are. It is also an opportunity for them to receive affirmation from the group.

DIRECTIONS:

1. Give a copy of the *BUILDING BLOCKS* handout to each child. Have pencils, crayons or magic markers available if needed.

2. Read the directions aloud and give several examples:

   HONEST   I try to tell the truth.
   FRIENDLY   I like to be with people.
   WORRIED   I don't understand what's happening to my family.

3. Tell them that when they are finished, they can take a magic marker or a crayon and decorate their paper if they wish.

4. When everyone is finished, ask the children to share some of the things they have written.

5. Ask the other children if they have any positive words they would add to one another's building blocks and to give the reason for their choice.

BUILDING BLOCKS

Think about who you are and the words that describe you. Write one of these words in each of the blocks below. At the bottom of the paper tell why you chose each word. You might write HONEST — I try to tell the truth, or WORRIED — I don't understand what's happening in my family.

I'M HERE BECAUSE

MATERIALS NEEDED: *I'M HERE BECAUSE* handout, pencils

PURPOSE: To provide the opportunity for children to express their reasons for being in the group. Some of these reasons may be negative, and in talking about them, the child may feel better. In hearing the responses from others, their feelings about being present in the group and about their parents' divorce can be validated.

To give children an opportunity to express some of the problem areas in their lives and give them some ideas about what can be covered in their time together which they may not have realized.

To give the leader some indication of the issues needed to be discussed throughout the SUNRISE sessions.

DIRECTIONS: Give each child a copy of the handout.

On this paper you see a line before each phrase. I'd like you to put a check mark by each phrase which expresses your feelings or needs. When you are finished, we will take some time to share your responses with the group.

Give children plenty of time to complete the handout. Then invite *those who wish* to share their reasons for coming. This can be a time in which those who were reluctant to come may be willing to see that SUNRISE might be helpful to them.

Take time to name the issues with which the children wish to deal during the remainder of the SUNRISE sessions. You may want to make a permanent listing which can be added to at any time as the group faces new issues in their lives.

OR

Do the exercise orally by asking:

Why are you here? What do you want to talk about?

You might need to get them started by using the ideas from the handout.

I'M HERE BECAUSE

I'm here because . . .

_____ My mom/dad said I had to come.

_____ I want to talk to others whose parents are divorced.

_____ I'm curious about what will happen in this group.

_____ I want to know I'm not alone.

_____ Other _____

_____

_____

Things I'd like to talk about are . . .

_____ reasons why people get divorced

_____ my fear that the parent with whom I live will go away too

_____ my behavior in school

_____ if it's my fault

_____ why I feel like I do

_____ spending time with the parent I don't live with

_____ feeling lonely

_____ mom/dad dating

_____ mom/dad getting married to someone else

_____ feeling left out

_____ other _____

_____

_____

HERE I AM

MATERIALS NEEDED: None

PURPOSE: To recognize that because their parents are divorced, the children have some specific needs. This gives them an opportunity to begin to express these needs.

To build self-esteem by helping children realize that they have something to offer the others in the group.

DIRECTIONS: Use the following questions as a basis for discussion.

Each of you probably has different reasons for being here. Maybe you're here because your mom or dad said you had to come. Others might be here because you recognize that life has become more complicated since your parents have lived apart and you'd like an opportunity to sort things out.

Whatever your reasons, they are okay.

1. *Why did you come to this group?*

2. *Have you talked to anyone about your parents' divorce — friend, counselor, teacher, relative?*

3. *What can others in this group do for you?*

4. *What can you do for others in this group?*

5. *What are some things you need to change in your life?*

GUIDELINES

MATERIALS NEEDED: Newsprint or chalkboard, magic marker or chalk

PURPOSE: To provide order for the group
To create an atmosphere of trust and caring
To develop a way of dealing with problems before they happen.

DIRECTIONS: Talk to the children about the need for some guidelines to assure them that they will be respected in the group and so each will have an opportunity to share within the group.

We are going to be spending a great deal of time together in SUNRISE. To help us to accomplish our purpose of dealing with feelings, experiences and concerns regarding your parents' divorce, we need to establish some guidelines for the group.

The first one I'll suggest is <u>confidentiality</u>. We won't tell people outside this group what we hear from one another. We can certainly tell others what we have shared and dealt with. In most cases I will not tell anyone what you share in our SUNRISE group. But if you need other people to get involved so you won't get hurt, I will need to inform them. I will not do this without first talking to you.

Another guideline is <u>listening</u>. We listen because each person is important and we want to show such persons that we care about what they say.

Write these two guidelines on newsprint or the chalkboard. Encourage the children to suggest several other guidelines to add to the list.

Explain to the children that if they misbehave, this disturbs the whole group. So if they cause problems in the group, they will be sent to another part of the room to work alone — to write about or to draw their feelings or to read a book. Sometimes the topic is just too difficult for them to talk about, so moving to another part of the room allows them the opportunity to just listen.

A good way to help children express what they are feeling is to have them draw a "picture story," like those they see in a comic strip. Usually what they draw will indicate what they are experiencing.

WHAT I WANT FOR MYSELF

MATERIALS NEEDED: Paper, pencils, crayons or colored pencils

PURPOSE: To give children some specific things they want to accomplish during their participation in SUNRISE. This activity also gives them a sense of direction for the group.

DIRECTIONS: Introduce the exercise with something like the following:

I'm going to give each of you a piece of paper. Fold it in half. Above the folded line write what you hope to gain from our sessions together.

In case you can't think of anything, I'll give you a few ideas. You might have others of your own.

You might wish to have these or similar statements prepared ahead of time on a large piece of paper, or you could evoke responses from the children first and then see how they correspond to these listed below.
- To realize that it's O.K. to belong to a single parent family
- To feel good about myself
- To get along better in school
- To find ways to keep from being caught in my parents' fighting
- To accept the fact that my parents are divorced
- To realize that I'm not responsible for the divorce

Remember that some children might put down as a goal to get their parents back together. If this happens, take the opportunity to point out that divorce is a grown-up problem and only *they* can make these decisions about their lives. It might be appropriate here to talk about the children's feelings of being responsible for the ending of the marriage. However, this is dealt with in Section III.

Children may wish to decorate the top portion of the paper in some way to make it special. Tell them to leave the bottom portion free because it will be used at the end of SUNRISE.

Collect the goals (they have no names but children will recognize their decorations) which can be used again in Section VI.

I BELONG, I AM SPECIAL

MATERIALS NEEDED: Materials for drawings/poster/badges/banner

PURPOSE: To help children see that they are special and that they belong to this group.

DIRECTIONS: Take some time to talk about why the children are in this group. They all have something in common — their parents are divorced. Some children are embarrassed about this and have many other feelings which affect their sense of well-being and self-esteem.

Because they belong to the group, it is important to be present at each session when possible. There will be times that they feel they don't need the group, but they need to realize that their presence is important to the others in the group.

After talking about being special, give them some time to design a poster, a badge or just a drawing indicating that they are special or have them develop a group banner for their SUNRISE group.

MY CONTRACT

MATERIALS NEEDED:	Contract form
PURPOSE:	The contract is only to be used in special circumstances. If a child does not want to participate in the group and the parent insists, the contract can be used as an agreement between the child and his or her parent to try the group for a certain number of sessions.
	This can be helpful to those children who are afraid to risk coming to the group or who feel they are beyond such a group. It is not for the child with behavior problems.
	You might feel that the parent needs the contract to ensure that his or her child comes to the group each week.
DIRECTIONS:	Talk to the child and parent about the importance of the group. Encourage them to try the group for a few sessions. Communicate to the parent the importance for the child and for the group that he or she is present for each session. Have both parent and child sign the contract.

MY CONTRACT

I, _____, agree to participate in SUNRISE for _____ sessions. I understand that whatever is shared within the group remains there. However, I am free to share or not to share what I have dealt with in the group with anyone else. I agree to participate in SUNRISE as fully as possible. After _____ sessions, I can choose to leave the group or to remain part of it.

SIGNED BY

_____

_____ Parent

_____ Group Leader

BEGINNING

MATERIALS NEEDED: *JOURNAL WRITING* handout, personal notebook

PURPOSE: Journaling can be done by children twelve years old and older. It is a means by which they can reflect upon their experience and feelings in a way which can be healing while at the same time private.

DIRECTIONS: Encourage older children to obtain a notebook which they can decorate in any way they wish. The journal is like a diary in which they record their thoughts, feelings and experiences each day. It can serve as a means of helping them to sort out their reaction to their parents' divorce and to make some choices to move on with their life. They might also express themselves through poetry or art.

When using the journal, suggest that they find a quiet place where they can be alone. It is helpful to be relaxed before writing. This can be done by taking a few minutes to sit quietly with eyes closed, breathing in and out deeply.

Once they feel peaceful and relaxed, either they can begin writing/drawing whatever they wish or they can use the *JOURNAL WRITING* handout.

Children can be invited to share with the group any insights they have gained through their journal writing. However, they must be assured privacy so they do not need to share anything they write in their journal unless they choose to do so.

You will find that some children will not keep a journal or will not be honest in their journal for fear someone will read it. Help them to find ways to protect their writings from others.

BEGINNING

A journal is like a diary. This is your private book in which you keep a record of your thoughts, feelings, struggles, concerns and hopes regarding your parents' divorce. Use whatever mode of expression is most appropriate for you at the time. You might write stories or poetry. You can express yourself through art. You may want to write a dialogue between yourself and one of your parents or between your parents. You can direct your thoughts to God. You might choose the Journal Writing questions to answer directly or to use as a guide to give you some ideas to explore.

Find a safe place to keep your journal so no one else will read it. This will give you the freedom to express whatever you wish in whatever way you choose without the fear of someone else reading it.

1. Write about your feelings as you came into the SUNRISE group.

2. What were some of your feelings or reactions to what happened in the group?

3. What do you hope will happen as you participate in SUNRISE?

4. To feel better about yourself, what do you need to start doing?

5. What do you need to stop doing?

6. What do you want to continue doing?

7. Using crayons, paints or colored pencils, express your feelings in color.

8. Draw pictures which tell a story of how you feel.

CHANGES IN THE FAMILY

- To acknowledge the reality of parents' divorce
- To recognize that changes occur after divorce
- To recognize that divorce affects the entire family
- To look at behavior/feelings resulting from the divorce

In order to move through a growthful healing process, children need to acknowledge that their parents really are getting a divorce and will not be living together. This is a difficult step because it is the beginning of letting go of a way of life as they have known it.

Family: The focus of this section is on "Family." It is not unusual for children to feel they are no longer family when their parents divorce. Some of the exercises in this section assist children in identifying the new form their family has taken. They are still part of a family. It just looks different. Help the children realize that families take different shapes—two-parent, single-parent, multi-generational, etc.—yet each is still a family.

It will be helpful for you to listen carefully as children talk about their family in order to better understand their experience.

Some children seldom or never see or hear from the absent parent. Others have parents who share custody to varying degrees. You might find some children who pack up their suitcases every three and a half days or every week to spend "equal" time with each parent. Other children might remain at home, and it is the parent who packs up, leaving the house in which the other parent will live for a given time.

The more common form of child custody is

for a child to live with one parent and to spend the weekend or every other weekend with the non-custodial parent. These changes can be wonderful experiences for the children as they spend some significant time with each parent. However, these can also be stressful times filled with anxiety and conflict. A child might resent sharing mom with her new husband. If parents use the time with a child to be critical of the other parent, the child can be torn by feelings of loyalty and self-identity.

The non-custodial parent, often the father, sometimes spends the time with their child as "the great entertainer," not knowing what else to do. Because the custodial parent often must assume the role of disciplinarian, a resentment can develop with a tendency to run to the non-custodial parent whenever things don't go well at home.

The custodial parent is often the brunt of their children's explosive feelings. They know this parent is always there for them and they are often not sure of the other parent.

Changes: With divorce come many changes. The loss of a parent, moving to a new neighborhood, and enrolling in a new school are tremendous changes in a child's life. There are also other changes which might be less obvious to children. Help them to notice changes within their family members—the way they dress, their behavior and mood swings. Under "Changes" in this section children will be given an opportunity to explore some of these changes and to see their interconnectedness with the divorce. This helps to objectify some of their feelings.

It is also well to look at change in general in order to realize that change is not necessarily bad. It is part of growth and part of being human. Some very positive things happen because we change.

Lead the children to an understanding that they cannot change other people. Most of all, they have no control over getting their parents back together again nor of the way their parents react to one another. They do have options to change their own negative behavior and attitudes. Help them to discover these options. As much as possible, evoke responses from them rather than giving them the answers you think they "should" have.

Looking at Divorce: One of the tasks for teenagers is to develop realistic hopes about relationships with the opposite sex. This is a difficult age for any child but it is certainly complicated by their parents' divorce.

In this section you will find "Looking at Divorce" topics which are designed to help them look more realistically at marriage and what is necessary for married love to grow and to nourish a relationship.

Rather than become distrustful and pessimistic of marriage because of their parents' divorce, children can use it as an opportunity to see what could have been done to better prepare for marriage as well as the importance of nurturing a marriage from the very beginning.

You may want to save this part for later in the SUNRISE program after they have dealt more directly with their feelings.

FAMILY PICTURE

MATERIALS NEEDED: Paper, magic markers, crayons or colored pencils

PURPOSE: It is sometimes difficult for children to express themselves, especially younger ones. In drawing they can show much through facial expressions and spatial relationships. The way they position people might give some indication of family relationships, i.e. if the non-custodial parent is remarried and has a family, the child might draw both families and put self with both.

The picture can be used as a basis for beginning to share with the group about their family. By sharing this with one another they will begin to realize that others have similar family configurations. Therefore, they are not alone. Always keep in mind their need to ·be affirmed in their family structure.

DIRECTIONS: Give each child a piece of paper. Have other materials and extra paper available as needed.

Here is a piece of paper. Use it to draw a picture of your family. If anyone needs extra paper it is here.

When they are finished, ask the children to show their picture to the group and to introduce their family. You may want to ask questions to bring out more information.

1. *Do you spend time with both of your parents?*

2. *With which parent do you live? What do you do when you are with your other parent?*

3. *What do you enjoy doing with your family?*

4. *Do you include grandparents, aunts, uncles, cousins as part of your family? What kinds of things do you do with them?*

Some children have little or no contact with the non-custodial parent, so it is important to be sensitive to this. Sometimes there is a great deal of pain and/or anger about this.

Children need to know that they are loved by both parents in the best way that their parents are able to love them. Sometimes a parent is unable to show his or her love.

FAMILY PORTRAIT

MATERIALS NEEDED: *FAMILY PORTRAIT* handout, pencils, crayons

PURPOSE: To reinforce the concept that divorce does not destroy the family. It merely takes on a different form.

DIRECTIONS: Give each child a copy of the handout. Read the directions with them.

Provide time for children to draw their picture and to identify family members. For younger children who cannot write their names, do not use the handout. Give them a large piece of paper on which to draw their family.

Take time for each child to show his or her picture to the group and to introduce the family.

FAMILY PORTRAIT

Draw a picture of your family in the picture frame. Write their names below and tell their relationship to you.

THE _____ FAMILY
(your last name)

HOME SEARCH

MATERIALS NEEDED: *HOME SEARCH* handout or flipchart/chalkboard, magic marker/chalk

PURPOSE: To acknowledge that just as there are different kinds of families so are there a variety of places that people call Home.

To invite children to express what it is like in their home.

DIRECTIONS: Give each child a copy of the *HOME SEARCH* handout (or do the exercise orally by asking them to see how many different kinds of homes they can think of. List them on a chalkboard or flipchart).

Read the directions with the children and then allow sufficient time for them to write their responses.

Invite the children to share with the group the various types of homes in which they have lived. Those who are comfortable doing so can share what it is like to live where they do. This might be a general or a more personal response. Be prepared to refocus the discussion if the sharing becomes too personal and/or inappropriate.

If children have lived in several different kinds of homes, ask them to talk about their favorite one and why they selected that particular one. It might be because their family was together or there was less conflict, or they might just have a silly answer which is all right.

ANSWER KEY

1. tapmernta	apartment	10. toelh	hotel
2. lowgnabu	bungalow	11. ohesu	house
3. unksebohu	bunkhouse	12. ohesutaob	boathouse
4. abnic	cabin	13. tuh	hut
5. tleasc	castle	14. ionnams	mansion
6. tagecot	cottage	15. lembio emoh	mobile home
7. pxeldu	duplex	16. tenpoheus	penthouse
8. taeste	estate	17. chnar	ranch
9. souherafm	farmhouse	18. entt	tent

HOME SEARCH

Families live in different types of homes. Below you will find some scrambled words. Each one is a place where people can live. Unscramble each of the words and circle those where you have lived.

1. tapmernta __ __ __ __ __ __ __ __ __

2. lowgnabu __ __ __ __ __ __ __ __

3. unksebohu __ __ __ __ __ __ __ __ __

4. abnic __ __ __ __ __

5. tleasc __ __ __ __ __ __

6. tagecot __ __ __ __ __ __ __

7. pxeldu __ __ __ __ __ __

8. taeste __ __ __ __ __ __

9. souherafm __ __ __ __ __ __ __ __ __

10. toelh __ __ __ __ __

11. ohesu __ __ __ __ __

12. ohesutaob __ __ __ __ __ __ __ __ __

13. tuh __ __ __

14. ionnams __ __ __ __ __ __ __

15. lembio emoh __ __ __ __ __ __ __ __ __ __

16. tenpoheus __ __ __ __ __ __ __ __ __

17. chnar __ __ __ __ __

18. entt __ __ __ __

Which kind of home is your favorite? _____

Why? _____

_____

_____

MY FAMILY IS SPECIAL

MATERIALS NEEDED: Copies of *MY FAMILY IS SPECIAL* handout unless you choose to do the exercise orally.

PURPOSE: Children from divorced families tend to look at their family as "broken," incomplete, different. They need to realize that:

1. There have always been single-parent families as a result of death, divorce, desertion, immigration, etc.

2. Just because parents are divorced does not make the family "broken." It might be more "together" than before the divorce.

3. Family is made up of those people to whom we are related by blood or adoption who love us in a special way. This includes people with whom we don't live.

This exercise is designed to help children obtain a broader concept of family by realizing that there are different kinds of families.

1. two parents and children

2. one parent and children

3. one parent and children part-time and the other parent and children part-time

4. children with grandparents and one parent

5. children with grandparents/aunt/uncle, etc.

6. blended family—one parent, children, stepparent, stepparent's children, children born to parent and stepparent

DIRECTIONS: Give the children the *MY FAMILY IS SPECIAL* handout or present the questions orally in an informal manner.

In the discussion try to include some of the concepts given above.

MY FAMILY IS SPECIAL

1. What is a family?

2. Can people still be family and live in different places? Why?

3. Who are the people in your family?

4. What are some special times your family celebrates? Who takes part in these family times?

5. Write a recipe for family. Include the necessary ingredients and directions for blending.

MY EXPERIENCE OF FAMILY

MATERIALS NEEDED: *MY EXPERIENCE OF FAMILY* handouts, pencils or chalkboard/ flipchart, chalk/magic marker

PURPOSE: To enable children to acknowledge their experience of family, their participation in it, and responsibility to their family.

Some children think that because their parents are divorced, they are no longer a family. They need to discover over and over that they are still family but a different kind of family.

DIRECTIONS: Questions can be asked verbally. Using a chalkboard or flipchart, you can evoke responses: For me home is . . .

If you use the handouts, have the children move to different parts of the room where they can have private space and not be distracted by the others.

Allow sufficient time for them to answer the questions. Then bring them together in a close circle. Invite them to share their responses. If they hesitate, you can begin by sharing your experience or by asking a question.

Discussion can include talking about ways in which children can help to bring about the kind of communication needed within a family so that it is a happier place for everyone.

MY EXPERIENCE OF FAMILY

For me home is:

_____ food	_____ maid service
_____ my bedroom	_____ where I am happy
_____ my hideaway	_____ a place to play
_____ where I am safe	_____ where I bring my friends
_____ where I feel accepted	_____ warm hugs
_____ a building	_____ where I don't fit in
_____ mom/dad	_____ TV
_____ a place to avoid	_____ other _____

My family is important to me because _____

Two things I could do to make my family life more pleasant are

_____

_____

Two things I like best about my family are

_____

_____

Two people who are important to me are _____

and _____

because

_____

_____

_____

_____

(OVER)

If I could really say what I want to say to each member of my family, it would be (list each member and what you'd say).

_____
_____
_____
_____
_____
_____
_____
_____
_____
_____
_____
_____
_____
_____
_____
_____

MY! LOOK HOW I'VE CHANGED

MATERIALS NEEDED: *MY FAVORITE THINGS* handouts or *SELF PORTRAIT* from "Getting to Know You" in Section I, pencils, crayons

PURPOSE: Children have already talked about their favorite things and/or drawn a self-portrait, describing them now. As they talk about change, it is helpful for them to look back in their life to see how they have changed in their interests and in their appearance.

In doing this help them to realize that change is happening all the time and necessary for their growth.

DIRECTIONS: Have the children list their favorite things when they were several years younger and/or draw a picture of themselves as they would have looked four or five years earlier. Have them compare these with *MY FAVORITE THINGS* from Section I. Lead them in a discussion of the importance of changes in their lives and the realization that what was important at one time changes as they grow older.

SOME THINGS ARE DIFFERENT NOW

MATERIALS NEEDED: None

PURPOSE: This exercise is another way to invite children to begin talking about what is different in their lives since their parents' divorce. As they share their experience with other children, they realize that they are not alone and can begin supporting and encouraging one another.

Children might not have made the connection between their parents' divorce and the changes that have taken place in their attitude, behavior and feelings.

In talking about their desire to reunite their parents, it is important for them to realize that just as they were not responsible for the divorce, neither do they have any control over getting their parents back together. They need to face the reality that their family life will be different than it was before the divorce.

DIRECTIONS: Introduce this section by talking about change. Relate it to the exercise, "My Favorite Things" from Section I.

Point out that the kind of toys, clothes, music, food, etc. they liked as a small child changed as they got older and that change was good. Change does not have to be bad. It's just different from what we are used to.

Evoke dialogue by using some of the following:

1. *How are things different at home since your parents' divorce?*
2. *What happens when you go home at night that is different?*
3. *How often do you see your "other" parent (the parent with whom you don't live)? How are these times for you?*
4. *How are things different for you at school?*
5. *What do you wish most? (Children will probably wish their parents were together again. Be sure to talk about how this just isn't possible.)*
6. *What have you done to try to get your parents together again? (Help them let go of this.)*
7. *What are you doing to make things run more smoothly in your family?*

CHANGES IN MY LIFE

MATERIALS NEEDED: *CHANGES IN MY LIFE* handout, pencils

PURPOSE: To help children focus on four consequences of their parents' divorce:

1. Not only does a child lose a parent, but there is a loss of the image of what family should be and what he or she assumes everyone else has—two parents. In preparation for the section on the grief process children need to realize that the divorce has brought about a number of significant losses in their lives which affect their feelings and behavior and which need to be grieved.

2. Not only are the changes external but there is also change within the child which he or she may not recognize or relate to the divorce. This helps the children to focus on their changed behavior and enables them to make some choices about how they want to behave.

3. Children of all ages attempt to bring their parents back together. Responding to these questions can help the children realize that this is a natural thing for them to do. It provides the opportunity for an open discussion on the reality of their parents' divorce and the realization that there is nothing they can do to reunite them.

4. Looking at things the children want to change in their own life opens discussion to those things which they do have within their power to change. In some cases this may require them to develop some assertiveness skills such as those found in "Giving 'I' Messages," Section V. You might choose to use that exercise at this time.

DIRECTIONS: Give children the *CHANGES IN MY LIFE* handout. Encourage them to be honest with themselves and to add to the sections marked "other."

After giving sufficient time for children to respond to the handout, open the discussion by asking if anyone would like to address a particular statement. If they find it difficult to share their responses, then move into a more general discussion, using the information above to evoke a more objective response.

OR

Ask the questions orally from the *CHANGES IN MY LIFE* handout.

CHANGES IN MY LIFE

1. Since my parents' separation/divorce, I have experienced the following changes in my life:

   _____ two parent family   _____ relationship with mom/dad

   _____ family vacations   _____ familiar family routines

   _____ friends   _____ money

   _____ school   _____ different home

   _____ other _____

2. I have noticed the following changes in myself:

   _____ a tendency to worry about my parents

   _____ sick or not feeling well more often than usual

   _____ a need to take care of mom/dad

   _____ withdrawing from my friends

   _____ increased fighting, clowning and/or disrupting the class

   _____ resignation from school activities

   _____ choosing different friends

   _____ other _____

3. I have tried to get my parents together again by:

   _____ promising to do better in school

   _____ taking on more responsibility at home

   _____ praying—but God doesn't seem to listen

   _____ behaving badly

   _____ other _____

4. Some things I would like to change in my life:

   _____ the way I feel about myself

   _____ the bad feelings I have about my parents' divorce

   _____ the way mom and dad talk about each other

   _____ the way I get caught in my parents' disagreements

   _____ my relationship with my friends

   _____ other _____

CHANGES IN MY FAMILY

MATERIALS NEEDED: *CHANGES IN MY FAMILY* handout, pencils

PURPOSE: To help children make connections between changes they have observed in themselves and in family members since their parents have separated or divorced. This enables them to be a bit more objective about these changes rather than taking them personally.

In looking at their own behavior children can begin to realize that they do have choices regarding *their own* behavior, disposition, dress, and relationships, and to explore the options they have to bring about these changes.

DIRECTIONS: Lead children to understand that divorce affects them in many ways. They cannot change other people but they can change their own behavior.

Give each child the handout and allow sufficient time for his or her thoughtful response in a private space. When finished, invite any insights or general response the children care to make.

CHANGES IN MY FAMILY

List the names of your family members below. After each name write the changes you have seen in each person since your parents were separated or divorced. This might include changes in behavior, disposition, dress, relationships, etc. Then tell what effect these changes have had on you.

FAMILY MEMBER	CHANGES I'VE NOTICED	EFFECT ON ME
_____	_____	_____
_____	_____	_____
_____	_____	_____
_____	_____	_____

You cannot change others but you can make those choices necessary to change things for yourself. Is there anything you want to change in your behavior, disposition, dress, relationships, etc.? What can you do to bring about these changes?

CHANGES FOR MYSELF	WHAT I NEED TO DO TO CHANGE
_____	_____
_____	_____
_____	_____
_____	_____

CHANGE ON!

MATERIALS NEEDED: *CHANGE ON!* handout, pencils

PURPOSE: To acknowledge the inevitability of change

To recognize that some of these changes are negative and some are positive and that's O.K.

DIRECTIONS: This exercise can be introduced by talking about change as a necessary part of life. Some changes we like and some we don't.
- change in seasons
- change in size as we get older
- change in temperatures

Give each child a copy of the *CHANGE ON!* handout. Read through the directions with them. Allow sufficient time for them to respond.

Invite them to share whatever they are comfortable sharing with the group. As they talk about changes they would like to make, help them to look at the options they have for making these changes.

CHANGE ON!

As time goes by, both you and your family change. Complete the chart below to show the changes that have already taken place. Then write the changes that will probably take place in the future.

Changes in the Last Year

1. _____

2. _____

3. _____

Possible Changes in the Next Year

1. _____

2. _____

3. _____

Changes I Would Like to Make Now

1. _____

2. _____

3. _____

List some things you do now that will cause changes in you and in your family. Circle those you feel will cause good changes and draw a line through the ones you feel will cause bad changes.

_____

_____

_____

_____

_____

WHY DIVORCE?

MATERIALS NEEDED: Newsprint and magic marker or chalkboard and chalk

PURPOSE: This is an activity for older children who are looking at their own relationships. As they begin to look at their own future, they are often fearful of marriage. They don't want to experience the pain which they've had in their own families.

When children can look at divorce more objectively, they can see some of the things about which they need to be aware in arriving at a commitment to marriage. Hopefully they will get the help needed when warning signs first emerge in their marriages.

DIRECTIONS: As an open discussion question, ask why children think people get divorced. Record responses on newsprint or the chalkboard. Try to evoke the following responses:

      a. married too young
      b. married because of a pregnancy
      c. few interests in common
      d. mental or emotional problems
      e. fighting
      f. financial difficulties
      g. infidelity
      h. alcoholism/drugs
      i. husband/wife/child abuse
      j. growing in two different directions

Develop each issue mentioned by children to help them see the need to get counseling or learn skills in communication or whatever it takes to keep the marriage alive. Help them realize that marriage is hard work, but well worth the effort.

You may want to have this exercise in one of the early sessions and repeat it again at greater depth toward the end.

WHY PEOPLE MARRY

MATERIALS NEEDED: Chalkboard and chalk or newsprint and magic marker

PURPOSE: To help late teens become aware of some unhealthy reasons to marry which could lead to marriage problems and possibly to divorce. This awareness can lead to a discussion of mature reasons for marrying.

DIRECTIONS: In talking about divorce, people often ask why it happened. Sometimes it is more helpful to ask why people married.

Elicit from the group some unhealthy reasons for getting married such as:

- *loneliness*
- *the need for the other person to make me happy*
- *to escape from an unhappy and/or abusive parental home*
- *the need to take care of someone or to be taken care of*
- *pregnancy which usually involves direct or indirect pressure to marry*
- *"We're in love" is not enough to sustain a marriage*
- *"He/she will change"*

After discussing each item, move into a discussion of some positive, mature reasons for getting married such as:

- *"We're in love and want to share a life together with a sense of permanence and commitment to one another and to the relationship."*
- *have good reasons that the marriage can endure*
- *adequate financial basis*
- *while still connected to family, have a sense of completeness as separate from family*
- *sense of independence on the part of both persons who are willing to blend two whole persons into an interdependent union. YOU and I become WE.*
- *can count on the other as an equal partner, not "In time he or she will grow up, will stop drinking, etc."*

CHANGES

Remember that your journal is just for you and that these questions are merely a guide in helping you to express your feelings about your experience. Use whatever way of expression is most comfortable for you—straight answers, poetry, conversation, art.

1. What changes have taken place in your life since your parents' separation and divorce?

2. What positive things have happened in the past month?

3. What negative things have happened in the past month?

4. What are some of the things you'd like to say to your mother and/or your father? Prepare a plan of action as to how you could do this or write a letter telling them how you feel. (You don't have to mail the letter unless you wish to do so. The important part is that you have some way of expressing your feelings.)

5. What are some things you enjoy doing? How can you continue doing at least some of these things? What are you doing or not doing that needs to be changed?

6. Write about some changes that have taken place at various times in your life which turned out to be positive. For example: You may not have wanted to move from your old neighborhood, but if you hadn't, you would never have met the person who is now your best friend.

SECTION III

WE ALL HAVE FEELINGS

- To understand that feelings are neither good nor bad
- To identify and acknowledge specific feelings
- To seek ways of dealing with these feelings

Many children have learned to suppress feelings. They are taught that it is bad to be angry. Others have grown up in homes where anger, violence and abuse are a way of life. Feelings are not dealt with in a direct, positive, healthy manner.

This section is one to which you will return often throughout the SUNRISE sessions as children become better able to talk about and to express their feelings. Use it as a guide for yourself so that you can better understand the children in your group.

Feelings: The exercises in this section marked "Feelings" are designed to help children acknowledge and express feelings which are a part of their everyday experience—winning a game, the death of a pet, going to the dentist. In the process they begin to realize that feelings are neither right nor wrong. Rather, it is how they respond to these feelings that can be harmful to themselves or to others.

Naming feelings helps children realize that others have similar feelings or that an identical situation can evoke different feelings. Sara is sad when it rains because she can't go out and play. Billy is excited because he knows that when it stops, he can go out and splash around in the puddles.

Feelings and My Parents' Divorce: Sometimes children don't make a connection between how they feel and their parents' divorce. Or they might not have names for these feelings. This section helps children talk about those feelings which are the consequence of the situation in which they find themselves.

Some children, especially older ones, are embarrassed by their parents' divorce and sometimes by their behavior. They attempt to cover up their true feelings. By naming some specific situations, children can talk about the feelings that are evoked.

This is a section which calls for patience, understanding, empathy and creativity on the part of the SUNRISE leader. Choose those modes of expression which are appropriate for the ages of the children in your group. Whether through art, story telling, role playing, puppets or direct discussion, try to aid the children in identifying and accepting their feelings. Older children can pretend they are conducting a TV talk show and interview one another about their experience.

The feelings of children will vary in kind and degree depending upon their situation. However, these are some of the feelings you can expect.

Guilt. It is not unusual for children of any age to feel responsible for their parents' divorce. They can usually pinpoint something they did wrong which "was the reason mom/dad left."

Anger. Children might express anger toward their parent(s), teachers, friends. In the process they alienate themselves from everyone around them. Basically, their anger is a response to their loss and the consequences of their new lifestyle. It is fueled by their confusion and their inability to express and make sense out of what is happening in their lives.

Often at least one parent is so caught up in his or her issues and pain that children feel a need to call attention to themselves. Direct and indirect expression of anger can be a way for a child to become the center of attention. It is a way of saying, "Look, everyone, I'm here. I hurt. I'm afraid." Or the anger might be a reaction to behavior and/or decisions of their parents(s) such as dating and remarriage.

Children are much more likely to act out their anger in the presence of the custodial parent who they know is there on a daily basis, than toward the non-custodial parent whom they see on occasion.

Abandoned. Some non-custodial parents choose to break all ties with their previous life, including their children. Children can wait for months and even years hoping, longing, dreaming and believing that the absent parent will call, write or visit them. When the reality finally strikes, the child may need to face not only feelings of anger but those of feeling abandoned and unloved.

Unloved. Children are often unable to understand that divorce is an adult problem. As a result, they not only feel rejected by the non-custodial parent but also unloved. This can have consequences as children grow older and are unable to trust anyone in a relationship.

Fear. If one or both parents communicate directly or indirectly that there might not be enough money for food and clothing, children can become obsessed by fear. When the custodial parent leaves home for an evening out, younger children can become terrified that this parent will not return. Older children might run away from home, thinking, "I'm not giving you a chance to leave me. I'll leave you first."

Listen carefully to the children in your SUNRISE group. You will learn a great deal about their experience, situations with which they struggle, and their pain. It is in listening that you will discover some feelings and reactions of the children. Remember the agreement of confidentiality. If you find it necessary to talk to someone else so that the child will not get hurt, first let the child know that this is necessary. Otherwise you break the trust the child has placed in you.

Dealing with Feelings: Often children don't realize that their behavior is related to what they feel inside. This section begins by exploring feelings which children experience in the process of growing up such as winning a ball game or receiving a poor grade in a test. Have them talk about these normal, nonthreatening experiences. Help them to name the feelings and to recognize the consequences of their behavior.

From here lead children to talk about the situations they face as a result of their parents' divorce and how a particular feeling affects their behavior. This may move you into some of the issues discussed in Section V.

It is especially important for older children to realize that they can't change others but they do have the choice to change their own behavior. Help them to explore options for responding to various situations and feelings.

This is a most appropriate time to use role playing. For younger children, use puppets, art expression and story-telling.

FEELINGS: NEITHER RIGHT NOR WRONG

MATERIALS NEEDED: Optional depending on how the topic is approached—paper plates, large white paper, crayons, magic markers

PURPOSE: Most often children are not able to identify how they feel. It is helpful to provide some experiences for them in which they can begin to look at both positive and negative feelings which are common to their everyday life.

They need to realize that feelings are neither right nor wrong. It's what they do with them that is important. It is the consequences of the feelings that can be positive or negative.

DIRECTIONS: Your own creativity and the age of the children will set the direction for this exercise. Some suggestions are listed below:

1. Children can role play or pantomime their feelings in the following situations. (Voice inflection, facial expression, and gestures are some indications of the intensity of a feeling.) Or they can just talk about similar experiences they have had, how they felt and how they expressed their feelings.
   - when people laugh at me
   - when I get a good grade on a test
   - when I find something important I've lost
   - when I'm caught doing something wrong
   - when I can't find someone to do something with me
   - when I'm planning something that's fun
   - when no one will talk to me
   - when it's the last day of school

2. Each child could choose a specific feeling and draw a picture of a face expressing this feeling on a paper plate or on a large piece of paper.

sad	worried	lonely
confused	glad	afraid
embarrassed	excited	angry
relaxed	happy	ashamed

3. The above situations could be acted out through the use of hand puppets.

SOMETIMES I FEEL

MATERIALS NEEDED:　　*SOMETIMES I FEEL* handouts, pencils (optional: clay or small paper plates, crayons/magic markers)

PURPOSE:　　This is an exercise designed to help children identify some feelings which are most common by using non-threatening, everyday situations.

Sometimes children don't have the vocabulary to describe what is going on inside of them at both happy and sad times in their life.

DIRECTIONS:　　Read the directions with the children. The words listed at the bottom of the handout are merely to be a help. They may use totally different words to fill in the blanks.

When they have finished talking about the various feelings they may have, affirm whatever they feel. This helps them to be comfortable expressing their feelings. This also helps them to understand that it is all right and natural to have feelings.

It is helpful for children to see that the same situations can evoke different feelings in different persons. One child may be delighted to have a free day from school while another may be disappointed. You may also wish to invite the children to give examples of times that they have had particular feelings. This might be a time they begin to talk about divorce-related feelings.

OR

Give each child some clay to make faces with different expressions. Invite the children to talk about these feelings.

OR

Give each child a small paper plate and magic marker or crayons. Ask the children to draw a face on each side of the plate. Each face is to show a different feeling—sad, excited, afraid, disappointed, etc.

Each child can then put the paper face in front of his or her face like a mask and tell a story to the group about this person he or she has become. These plates can be used for story-telling throughout the SUNRISE sessions.

SOMETIMES I FEEL

We all have different feelings at different times. Some of these are happy feelings. Some are sad. Some are mad and some are glad. How do you feel?

I FEEL . . .

_____ when I'm alone in the dark.

_____ when someone teases me.

_____ when I lose something important to me.

_____ when no one pays any attention to me.

_____ when I've done something wrong and I don't want anyone to know.

_____ when I'm chosen to do something special.

_____ when I have a fight with my friend.

_____ when I win a game.

_____ when it's my birthday.

_____ when I go to the dentist.

_____ when I succeed at something which has been very hard.

_____ when I don't know what to do or say.

_____ when my pet dies.

_____ when we have a free day from school.

Some feelings you might have are:

anxious	sad	angry
happy	excited	lonely
afraid	disappointed	embarrassed
proud	guilty	ashamed

HOW I FEEL

MATERIALS NEEDED: Paper plates or drawing paper, magic marker, or crayon (materials needed will depend on the way you do this exercise), feeling words

PURPOSE: To help children identify more specifically those feelings which are directly related to their parents' divorce. In so doing they can begin to talk about why they feel as they do. They can make connections between their feelings and what is happening in their lives.

Remember that feelings are neither good nor bad. It's reacting to these feelings by hurting ourselves or others that can be harmful.

DIRECTIONS: On a chalkboard or on a poster prepared ahead of time, list some feeling words (children can add to this list). For example:

Young children
happy   angry   sad   okay   afraid

Older children

angry	abandoned	embarrassed	unloved
afraid	worried	confused	guilty

Have children do any of the following:
- Draw a face on a paper plate or on paper showing the feelings they have felt.
- On a piece of paper write one of the feeling words. Draw that feeling with crayons. Use a different paper for each feeling.
- Using the How I Feel Teacher's Guide have the children hold up their feeling drawing for each situation mentioned. For example:

1. *How do you feel when you can't see one of your parents?*

2. *If you feel that nobody cares, what does that feel like?*

3. *How do you feel about your mother or your father dating?*

Children might have much different feelings about the same situation. Have them talk about why they feel the way they do and how this affects their behavior at home and in school.

HOW I FEEL TEACHER'S GUIDE

Below are listed some situations which children experience. Next to them are suggested feelings as a guide for you. They might not be the way each child feels. Give them the situation and let them show their feeling picture and/or talk about how they feel in these situations.

SITUATION	POSSIBLE FEELINGS
I can't see mom/dad very often.	Anger
So many things have changed.	
Mom/dad is gone so much.	
Mom/dad doesn't care.	Abandoned/Unloved
Nobody cares.	
Nobody listens to me.	
I don't fit in any place.	
Mom/dad is dating someone else.	
My parents are divorced.	
Mom/dad acts/dresses differently.	Embarrassed
I don't know why my parents got divorced.	Confused
I don't know what's happening to me.	
I wonder what will happen to me/us.	Worried/Afraid
Sometimes we don't have enough money.	
I am afraid mom/dad will leave too.	
I wonder if the divorce is my fault.	Guilt

Don't rush this activity. Spend time discussing each situation. Children can suggest many other situations and a variety of feelings. This is a good activity to come back to now and then as children come in touch with more of their feelings and feel more comfortable talking about them.

FEELING FACES

MATERIALS NEEDED: *FEELING FACES* handout, pencil magic marker or crayons

PURPOSE: This is an activity which relates directly to the children's experience of divorce. By drawing the faces related to each feeling word, they begin to express those feelings which they have experienced.

DIRECTIONS: Give each child a copy of the *FEELING FACES* handout. Have them find a place in the room where they can work in privacy. Instruct them to draw a face for each feeling.

When they have completed their drawings, bring the children back together. Help them to talk about these feelings with questions like the following:

When do you feel angry?

What do you do when you feel afraid?

Why do you feel abandoned?

In talking about specific feelings you can begin to discuss positive ways of dealing with them.

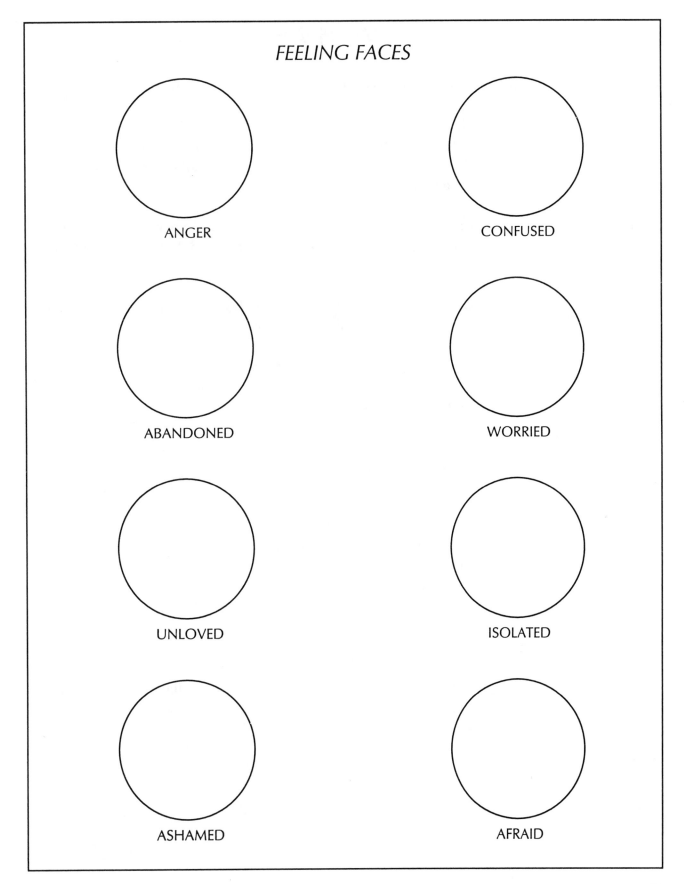

FEELING FACES

ANGER

CONFUSED

ABANDONED

WORRIED

UNLOVED

ISOLATED

ASHAMED

AFRAID

WHAT I DO WITH WHAT I FEEL

MATERIALS NEEDED: *WHAT I DO WITH WHAT I FEEL* handouts, pencils

PURPOSE: Children are usually not aware that certain behavior is the result of feelings which they have—both positive and negative. This exercise is designed to help children identify some of these behaviors and feelings in relation to specific situations.

DIRECTIONS: Give children the handout and ask them to respond to as many statements as they can. Don't be surprised if they are unable to articulate this in writing.

When children seem to be finished, go over the statements orally. As they begin to talk about the various situations, they may become more aware of their own responses. As they talk about the behavior, move beyond this to ask them how they would feel. In so doing they will begin to make a connection between their feelings and their behavior.

You can then ask them to add their own situations which may pertain more directly to their parents' divorce.

As the children talk about their response to a particular situation or feeling, help them to distinguish between healthy and unhealthy responses—those which hurt other people and those which don't.

EXAMPLE: When I am angry

Negative—talk back to other persons, yell at them or someone else, hit them, slam the door.

Positive—go outside and run, punch your pillow, play a game which takes lots of energy, play a musical instrument.

WHAT I DO WITH WHAT I FEEL

What would you do in the following situations?

• Your team just won the game. _____

• You can't find your completed math paper. _____

• Your mother calls you inside from play to clean your room. _____

• You receive an excellent grade on a difficult test. _____

• Your little brother/sister takes something which belongs to you. _____

• Your good friend moves far away. _____

• You have no friends. _____

• When no one seems to care _____

• When you are treated unfairly _____

• When nobody seems to notice you _____

• When nothing seems to be right _____

• When you are praised _____

• When you feel left out _____

• When your mom/dad scolds you _____

• When you are very lonely _____

• When you are afraid _____

• When you feel guilty _____

• When you are angry _____

A LOOK AT MY FEELINGS

MATERIALS NEEDED: *A LOOK AT MY FEELINGS* handouts, pencils

PURPOSE: This activity can help older children take a deeper look at their feelings and their related behavior. The goal here is to lead children to discover alternative ways of responding to the situations in which they find themselves.

DIRECTIONS: Have children go to their private space to respond to the statements on the handout *A LOOK AT MY FEELINGS*. Give them adequate time.

Bring the group together and ask them to respond to anything they have written which they want to share. If nothing is said, you could ask some lead questions like:

When I get uptight about something, all my relationships seem to be affected. How do you react? What makes you uptight?

When I was young and there was fighting in the family, I would always run to my room and hide my head under the pillow. What do you do? What could you do that would be more helpful/ positive?

Leading questions in this way is more than asking questions. It is an identification with the children's experience which is important.

As the children talk about their experiences and feelings, guide them in finding options for their behavior which are positive and healthy rather than destructive to themselves and to others.

Conclude the sharing with the question:

What can you do to make life in your family happier?

A LOOK AT MY FEELINGS

Indicate your experience of the following:

I feel stressed out over:

_____	my parents' expectations	_____	money
_____	pressure from my friends	_____	school/teachers
_____	too much responsibility	_____	not enough responsibility
_____	difficulty talking to mom/dad	_____	my brothers/sisters
_____	things my parents say and do	_____	other _____

Sometimes when the stress is too great, I _____

_____

Sometimes I cut myself off from others.

How do I do this? What do I say or do? _____

_____

Whom do I cut off—family, friends, teachers? _____

_____

What can I do/say instead of cutting people off? _____

_____

Sometimes I feel lonely, isolated and left out.

How does this feel? _____

_____

What do I do when I feel this way? _____

_____

What are some positive things I could do/say when I'm feeling lonely, isolated or left out?

_____

Sometimes there is fighting in my family. At these times I:

_____	try to stop the fighting	_____	remain silent
_____	am right in the middle of it	_____	call a friend
_____	leave the house	_____	yell and scream
_____	hide my head under a pillow	_____	other _____

MY FEELINGS IN COLOR

MATERIALS NEEDED: Drawing paper, crayons

PURPOSE: Sometimes when feelings are bottled up inside, it's hard to put words on them. Or even if there are words, it's often difficult to describe the feeling.

This exercise helps children express their feelings in a visual, creative way.

These drawings can be used later for the exercise in Section VII, "From Darkness to Light."

DIRECTIONS: Give each child several pieces of paper and have more available in case they are needed. On one side of the paper have the children write a feeling such as:

- anger
- guilt
- sadness

Or they can write a situation which evoked a great deal of feeling such as:

- Mom and dad are getting a divorce.
- Dad moved out.
- Mom expects too much of me.

Then have them turn the paper over and give the following instructions:

Think about the feeling or situation you wrote on the other side of your paper. Then take the color of crayon or crayons which express how you felt. Draw that feeling on the paper. Your picture might be circles, lines scribbles or whatever best describes your feeling for you.

Press hard on the crayon so you have vivid, solid colors. Try to fill most of the paper with color.

When you are finished, take another paper and do the same with another feeling or situation.

When you feel the children have had sufficient time, invite them to show their pictures and to talk about them.

You might want to save the pictures for the children for use in Section VI, "From Darkness to Light."

LETTING FEELINGS OUT

MATERIALS NEEDED: Tape recorder or record player, music tape or record

PURPOSE: To express feelings in a relaxing, non-threatening manner. As children act as directors of an orchestra or pretend to be the musicians or even if they just listen, they begin to feel the music. This allows an outlet of expression for their own feelings.

DIRECTIONS: Choose an instrumental recording with various movements—dancing flute, clashing cymbals, rumbling drums, lyrical violins, etc. *The Grand Canyon Suite* is a good example.

Tell the children you are going to play some music and you want them to be the directors or they can pretend to play a particular instrument. Have them listen closely and try to feel the music as they direct or play. You can have them close their eyes if you wish.

OR

Choose music which expresses one particular feeling—scary, happy, angry, lonely, etc. Have children close their eyes and listen carefully to the music. Whichever mode of expression you use, when the music is finished, ask the children what the experience was like, what kind of feelings they experienced. Or you can say nothing and let the experience speak for itself.

FEELINGS

Remember, your journal is just for you. Express your thoughts and feelings as honestly as you can in the way you feel most comfortable.

1. When I think about my parents' separation/divorce I feel . . .

2. Choose a feeling such as anger, guilt, loneliness, rejection. Describe how that feeling looks and feels. Or express with color how it looks and feels. Talk to that feeling as though it were a person. Let it talk back to you as in a conversation.

3. Express through drawing how you feel about your parents' divorce or about how things are for you now. You may want to use a series of pictures which tell a story like a comic strip story.

4. Think about one feeling which seems to cause you the most difficulty. Describe how this feeling affects your behavior—how you act toward other people.

5. Sometimes when we don't want others to know how we feel, we pretend to feel a different way than we really do. This is like wearing a mask. Draw a picture of a mask you wear so others won't know how you really feel. Write a conversation that this mask would have with your real feelings.

6. Feelings are neither good nor bad. It's what we do with them that can cause some difficulty. What are some of the ways that you can express how you feel without hurting someone else? (Example: Anger—run, play tennis/football, punch a pillow).

7. If you could sit down with your mother and/or your father right now, what would you want to tell them about how you feel . . .
   . . . about yourself
   . . . about them
   . . . about your future
   . . . about _____

SECTION IV

THE GRIEF PROCESS

- To understand the natural process of grief
- To recognize the symptoms of grief/loss
- To see the relationship between behavior and grieving

Anyone who experiences a significant loss goes through a period of grief. SUNRISE uses the grief process developed by Dr. Elisabeth Kübler-Ross[1]—denial, anger, bargaining, depression and acceptance. It is important that the SUNRISE leader understand the grieving process.

The Grief Process and Me: In this section is a detailed description of the grief process as it relates to the feelings and reactions of children. Within these stages falls the entire range of feelings, often expressed as anger and depression which includes guilt, loneliness, fear, rejection, feeling unloved, embarrassed and confused. Knowing the stages of grief will help you as the SUNRISE leader to better understand that the feelings expressed by the children in your group are a normal response to their grief.

Depending on the personality of the child and their particular situation, the duration and intensity of grieving varies. The process is not necessarily a smooth one. Children can accept their situation one day and the next day deny it. They move back and forth within the grieving process as they deal with their loss.

Some children might get stuck along the way. The child who denies the reality of his or her parents' divorce is responding normally. However, if this continues for months, he or she might need encouragement to face the reality so as to be able to continue to move through the grieving process.

Dealing with Grief: The whole purpose of SUNRISE is to provide a safe environment in which children can deal with their grief, letting go of their negative feelings and finding ways to cope. In doing this it is hoped that they will be able to accept their situation and to grow in their acceptance of themselves and their sense of self-esteem. These activities offer ways of dealing with the grief process for various age levels.

---

1. Elisabeth Kübler-Ross, *On Death and Dying*, New York: Macmillan, 1969.

THE GRIEF PROCESS AND ME GUIDE

When we lose something or someone we love very much, we grieve. Grieving is a natural process of healing an open wound.

	My Words	*My Actions*
DENIAL	"Mom/dad will come back home."	Happy on the outside to convince everyone and myself that all is well
	"I'm ashamed and don't want anyone to know what's happening to my family."	Keeping a distance from others so they won't ask questions
	"Things really weren't so bad before dad/mom left."	Keeping busy so I don't have to think about what has happened
ANGER	"What right do they have to break up our family? It isn't fair!"	Physical and verbal outbursts of anger
	"I hate everyone!"	Pushing people away
	"I don't like her/him. She/he made dad/mom leave!"	Blaming others
BARGAINING	"Dad/mom, please fix things up and I'll be home on time, study harder and help more around the house."	Attempt to do every thing right and well
	"Dear God, if you will bring my parents together again, I won't talk back to them anymore."	Attempt to bring parents together
DEPRESSION	"I'm so sad. My whole world is falling apart."	Silent and withdrawn from family, friends and activities

DEPRESSION *(continued)*	"It's my fault!"	Unable to concentrate or to study
	"I'm all alone. I trust no one. Everything seems so hopeless."	Can't sleep at night or tend to sleep all the time.
	"Nobody cares."	No interest in friends, hobbies, etc.
ACCEPTANCE	"I don't want my parents to be divorced, but that's the way it is. I am still loved and I have my own life to live."	Cheerful, friendly, confident Involved again in life around me
REACHING OUT	"I've been through a lot. I've felt hurt and I've struggled but I'm O.K. I'd like to help other kids who are going through a divorce."	Ability to reach out to others who have experienced divorce A sensitivity toward others who hurt
	"I feel good about myself. I'd like to get involved in things which will help others."	Getting involved in activities which help others

TALKING ABOUT GRIEF

MATERIALS NEEDED: Puppets—optional

PURPOSE: To present stories through which younger children can identify and talk about their experience.

DIRECTIONS: Below are several vignettes describing the various phases of the grief process—denial, anger, bargaining, depression, acceptance, reaching out.

Each story can be read directly, adapted by the story teller or told through use of puppets.

DENIAL

My name's Jenny. Daddy doesn't live at home anymore. Mom said that she and daddy are getting a divorce and that he won't be coming back here to live anymore. But I think she's wrong. Daddy wouldn't leave me. I know they used to fight a lot. I'd hide my head under the pillow so I wouldn't hear. I didn't like to hear them fight but every morning things seemed to be all right again. I think that maybe daddy just got mad like I do with my friends sometimes. We fight but we make up again. Daddy will be back. I don't want anyone to know that daddy is gone. I don't want people to know that we aren't a real family any more. I don't like people to ask me questions about him. But when they do, I just say, "Daddy is gone for a while but he'll be back."

1. What would you say to Jenny?

2. Do you sometimes feel like Jenny, thinking your mom or dad will come back home?

Evoke responses which deal with the following situations:

- feelings of fear or anger when parents don't get along

- divorce is not the same as a fight you have with a friend

- shame connected with the divorce

- just because mom or dad does not live at home does not mean you are not a "real" family

81

ANGER

Hi. I'm Billy. My mom and dad are divorced. I love both of them and don't see why they can't live together. I haven't seen dad for a long time and mom's no fun anymore.

I miss the times we had together as a family. At school I try to tell them how sad I am but they just laugh at me, so I just punch them good. It makes me feel better, but it also gets me into lots of trouble. No one seems to understand.

1. What would you say to Billy?

2. What could he do instead of punching people?

3. Do you sometimes feel so sad that you hurt other people? What could you do instead?

Evoke responses which deal with the following:

• We all feel angry sometimes and that's O.K. But it isn't O.K. to hurt other people.

• Other ways to deal with anger, i.e. running, biking, playing basketball (or anything which tires our body), punching our pillow, talking about what makes us angry.

BARGAINING

Hello. I'm Lucy. My mom and dad are divorced but I'm going to get them together again. All week I've been very good. I've helped with the dishes and have even made my bed without being told.

I have a little brother and he's a real pest. But I play with him and share my toys with him. I've been doing all my school work each night. I think mom and dad are noticing the change in me, so soon dad will come home again.

Before I go to bed at night I remind God how good I've been so he'll work things out for us.

1. What would you say to Lucy?

2. Do you try to get your parents back together again? Is it realistic to think you can?

Evoke responses which deal with the following:

- You are not responsible for your parents' divorce. It is something that happened between them.

- You cannot bring them together again no matter how hard you try.

- God hears our prayer and is with us and wants what is best for us, but he cannot bring your parents together unless they want to come.

DEPRESSION

I'm Oscar. I'm so sad because nobody loves me anymore. My mom hasn't lived with us for a long time. I worry about Dad—I'm afraid that someday he won't come home either and then I'll be all alone. I don't play with my friends anymore. Sometimes I just go in my room and bury my head under my pillow—and I cry. I know it's my fault that all this happened.

1. What would you say to Oscar?

2. In what ways have you felt like Oscar?

3. What do you do when you are sad?

4. Do you think you are to blame for your parents' divorce?

Evoke responses which deal with the following:

- Divorce happens between a husband and wife. You are not to blame.

- Just because your parents don't get along with each other does not mean they do not love you. They love you the best they can, which sometimes isn't enough.

- Mention ways children have of dealing with their feelings.

- Talk about their fear of losing the other parent.

ACCEPTANCE

They call me Sunshine because I'm happy most of the time. I wasn't always like this, though. When mom and dad were divorced, I was very sad and unhappy. Nothing seemed to be right.

But now I know that no matter what happens between them, they both love me. Sometimes they don't love me as much as I want, but that's O.K. I know they do the best they can.

1. Do you believe you are loved by both of your parents? How do you know?

2. Do you have some good times with both of them?

Evoke responses which deal with the following:

- Sometimes parents are hurting and can't love us as much as we want, but they love the best they can.

- Stress the importance of feeling at home with both parents if time is spent with both of them.

- Some children may seldom or never see one parent. Talk to them about the times in the past when they felt loved by that parent. Help them to see that this can't be taken away from them.

MY EXPERIENCE

MATERIALS NEEDED: Copies of *MY EXPERIENCE* handout, pencils for each child

PURPOSE: Identifying behavior helps children:

- To acknowledge their behavior

- To create a common bond of experience

- To understand that this behavior is a reaction to their parents' divorce and that they can choose other responses

- To realize that this is a normal part of a healing process

DIRECTIONS: Give each child a copy of *MY EXPERIENCE*. When people hurt, they say and do things that they don't really mean—even adults! Give the following directions:

I have given you a paper on which you will find words and actions that might describe your reaction to your parents' divorce. Check those which apply to you and then we'll talk about them.

Give children sufficient time for this exercise. Then talk about their responses in whatever order or way they wish to give them.

MY EXPERIENCE

THINGS I THINK OR FEEL

_____ "Mom/dad will come back home."

_____ "I'm ashamed and don't want anyone to know what's happening to my family."

_____ "Things really weren't so bad before dad/mom left."

_____ "What right do they have to break up our family? It isn't fair!"

_____ "I hate everyone!"

_____ "I don't like her/him. She/he made dad/mom leave!"

_____ "Dad/mom, please fix things up and I'll be home on time, study harder and help more around the house."

_____ "Dear God, if you will bring my parents together again, I won't talk back to them anymore."

_____ "I'm so sad. My whole world is falling apart."

_____ "It's my fault!"

_____ "I'm all alone. I trust no one. Everything seems so hopeless."

_____ "Nobody cares."

_____ "I don't want my parents to be divorced, but that's the way it is. I am still loved and I have my own life to live."

_____ "I feel good about myself. I'd like to get involved in things which will help others."

THINGS I DO

_____ happy on the outside to convince everyone and myself that all is well

_____ keep a distance from others so they won't ask questions

_____ keep busy so I don't have to think about what has happened

_____ physical and verbal outbursts of anger

_____ push people away

_____ blame others

_____ attempt to do everything right and well

_____ attempt to bring my parents together again

_____ silent and withdrawn from family, friends and activities

_____ unable to concentrate or to study

_____ can't sleep at night or tend to sleep all the time

_____ no interest in friends, hobbies, sports which I used to like

_____ cheerful, friendly confident

_____ involved again in life around me

_____ ability to reach out to others who have experienced divorce

_____ sensitivity toward others who hurt

_____ desire to get involved in activities which help others

THE GRIEF PROCESS AND ME

MATERIALS NEEDED:
Copies of THE GRIEF PROCESS AND ME guide for each person, chalkboard/chalk or poster paper/magic marker

PURPOSE:
To lead teens to an understanding that any significant loss must be grieved.

To help teens identify words they have said and actions they have done so that they can see that their reaction is part of the normal process of grief. Seeing the process before them helps them to realize that they are not alone in their experience.

DIRECTIONS:
First talk about other losses in the teens' lives—the death of a pet, a friend moving away, a broken relationship, changing schools, etc. Have them talk about their feelings and their reactions to these experiences. As they talk, place their responses under one of the grief process categories:

DENIAL   ANGER   BARGAINING   DEPRESSION   ACCEPTANCE

When finished, explain that this is the grief process through which we move after any significant loss. Then give each person a copy of THE GRIEF PROCESS AND ME guide. Together read through the descriptions and discuss. Take each section separately. Note that the feelings and reactions they are now having to their parents' divorce are similar to those of other losses.

MY EXPERIENCE OF THE GRIEF PROCESS

MATERIALS NEEDED: Copies of *MY EXPERIENCE OF THE GRIEF PROCESS* handout or THE GRIEF PROCESS AND ME guide, pencils

PURPOSE: It is good for teenagers to be able to put in writing their own experience of grief. Their reactions might be different from those given in the guide.

Time is provided for them to do some quiet reflecting about what has been happening in their lives and to begin to make sense out of it.

DIRECTIONS: Use only after a discussion of the grief process. Allow sufficient time for a written response. Then bring the group together to discuss their experiences of the grieving process.

MY EXPERIENCE OF THE GRIEF PROCESS

Denial:

Things I said

_____
_____
_____
_____

Things I did

_____
_____
_____
_____

Anger:

Things I said

_____
_____
_____
_____

Things I did

_____
_____
_____
_____

Bargaining:

Things I said

_____
_____
_____
_____

Things I did

_____
_____
_____
_____

(OVER)

Depression:

Things I said

_____

_____

_____

_____

Things I did

_____

_____

_____

_____

Acceptance:

Things I said

_____

_____

_____

_____

Things I did

_____

_____

_____

_____

Reaching Out:

Things I said

_____

_____

_____

_____

Things I did

_____

_____

_____

_____

COPING

Use THE GRIEF PROCESS AND ME guide as you write in your journal this week.

1. What are some of the things I say which indicate how I am coping with my loss?

2. What are some of the things I do which indicate how I am coping with my loss?

3. Choose one of the words in the left-hand column—denial, anger, bargaining, depression, acceptance, reaching out—which best describes how I am coping at the present time. Carry on a conversation as though it were a person.

4. Write a letter to an imaginary person my age whose parents are going through a divorce. What would I tell them about coping with the loss they feel?

5. Trace my movement through the different stages of coping with grief/loss.

SECTION V

ISSUES

- To explore some specific issues affecting children
- To help children learn to express their needs and their feelings in a direct and positive manner

Both adults and children play "games" to get what they want. These are special kinds of games. They are not fun. One person is usually controlling the situation while the other feels like the victim. Children use these "games" to manipulate their parent(s). Parents can consciously and unconsciously use their children to get back at their former spouse or to meet their own social and/or emotional needs. It takes two to play one of these games. In this section children learn to express their needs and feelings directly.

Throughout the SUNRISE sessions children will bring up numerous issues with which they must deal. Some of these situations leave children confused. Others may result in feelings of being used, ignored or discounted. As a consequence the feelings which surface might be expressed through negative behavior, passivity or non-direct responses. They might become people-pleasers in an effort to make life run more smoothly around them. Children who are hurting need to discover ways to cope.

SUNRISE children are taught to acknowledge situations which are stressful and to develop healthy ways of dealing with them. Listening to one another can be invaluable. Children realize that they are not alone in their experience, and they have the opportunity to develop more effective coping skills in a safe environment.

Dealing with Issues: The most important part of this section is to provide the opportunity for children to practice dealing with some of the issues which are a part of their daily life. By using puppets or role playing, children not only learn to acknowledge their needs but also to express them in a positive, non-threatening way to their parent(s).

Giving "I" messages is a most effective tool for both adults and children to use in expressing their needs and concerns. A description of this process is given in this section.

Issues for Adolescents: This section has been specifically developed for adolescents as a supplement to the preceding material. Their issues include moral questions and concerns about relationships and marriage.

GIVING "I" MESSAGES

MATERIALS NEEDED: None

PURPOSE: To enable children to learn to express their feelings and to deal with uncomfortable situations by giving "I" messages. This way of communicating can prevent defensiveness on the part of the other person. In owning their own feelings children will tend to talk more about their experience rather than give unnecessary details about their parents.

Children often get caught in the "games" their parents play with each other. Using "I" messages can be a non-threatening way for children to express their feelings about getting caught between their parents.

DIRECTIONS: Giving "I" messages is based on a process of acknowledging:
1. Behavior
2. Feeling
3. Consequence

Give the following directions:

Sometimes we feel hurt, angry, left out or upset by something another person says or does. It is difficult to tell them how we feel, so we often act out our feelings by yelling, hitting, saying things we really don't mean, or walking away.

In our SUNRISE group we will use "I" messages to talk about these feelings. Rather than blame other persons for something they say or do which we don't like, we will tell them

1. What we don't like by saying, "When you _____ (don't want to play with me) . . ."

2. What we feel by saying, "I feel _____ (angry/sad/rejected) . . ."

3. The reason we feel as we do by saying, "because _____ (I am left out of the fun) . . ."

Can you think of some situations in which you could use "I" messages?

REMEMBER: "When you_____ , I feel_____ , because _____ ."

Have the children suggest situations which they can role play, using "I" messages.

GAMES PARENTS PLAY

MATERIALS NEEDED:

Younger Children:
Puppets, *GAMES PARENTS PLAY* handout for leader

Older Children:
GAMES PARENTS PLAY handout for each child

PURPOSE:

Children find themselves in some awkward situations. They need to be able to talk about these times to discover that:

a. Other children have similar experiences.

b. The feelings they have about getting caught in these games are O.K.

c. There are ways in which they can communicate their feelings to their parents.

d. They might feel better after talking about a difficult situation they experience.

DIRECTIONS:

Use only after you have taught and practiced the "I" message skills.

Younger Children

Use puppets to set up the situations from the handout and/or any other experience the children might have talked about previously. Some questions could be asked to initiate response from the children such as:

1. *What would you say to someone who has had an experience like this?*

2. *Have you ever experienced anything like this? How did you feel? What did you do? Did you feel good about that? What else could you have done?*

As the children respond, they might want to take one of the puppets and let the puppet give the answer which is a little less threatening than a direct response.

Older Children

Using the *GAMES PARENTS PLAY* handout, similar questions as those above could be asked to initiate sharing.

OR

The situations could be cut apart and given to different children to role play. Each story could be expanded to include ways they might respond using "I" messages.

OR

They could pretend they are conducting a TV interview on how to deal with these uncomfortable situations.

GAMES PARENTS PLAY

1. When I spend the weekend with dad, he asks me all kinds of questions. He'll say, "Does your mother go out at night?" and "What does she say about me?" Then when I return home, mom asks the same kind of questions about him. I don't like getting caught in the middle. I feel like a spy.

2. Mom and dad are always saying things about each other and forcing me to take sides. I feel caught in a tug-of-war.

3. My mom keeps reminding me that I'm now the man in the house. She consults me on almost every decision she makes. Sometimes I like this because it makes me feel important. But then I think, "Gee, I'm just a kid!"

4. I like being with dad, but sometimes I feel more like the "mother" of the house. He expects me to clean the house, cook the meals and take care of the little kids. I don't mind doing this sometimes, but I'm just a kid myself!

5. Mom/dad is always buying me gifts and taking me places. It's fun and I like feeling so important, but I wonder if he or she can afford it.

6. I don't know what's gotten into dad. He's different. He looks and dresses much younger than he is and he treats me like his buddy. I'd just like him to be my dad.

7. Mom takes me to movies, restaurants and concerts all the time. It's fun but I hardly have time for my own friends.

8. Sometimes I feel so trapped. Mom keeps telling me that she doesn't know how she'd get along without me. I wonder if I'll ever be free to live my own life.

9. I look forward to the times I can spend with dad, but often mom won't let me see him because his girlfriend is there. This really makes me angry.

10. Sometimes dad refuses to give mom any child support money just because she doesn't spend it the way he thinks she should. I feel I'm the one who loses out.

11. I hate it when mom and dad tell me how bad the other one is. I wish they'd leave me out of their fights.

12. Does my mom ever get angry when dad brings me home too early or too late! I seem to be the cause of all their fighting.

13. I like spending the weekends with mom since I don't see her during the week. But it also means I don't have time to spend with my friends. I wish she would understand.

14. Sometimes my dad doesn't even show up when he has promised to take me some place. This makes mom pretty mad. Yet I'm the one who gets hurt.

GAMES KIDS PLAY

MATERIALS NEEDED: Chalkboard/chalk or poster paper/magic marker

PURPOSE: Children can be very much aware of how they get caught in their parents' games. They might not be quite as conscious of the ways they play games in order to manipulate their parents.

This activity helps the children:

1. To realize they are "playing games" to get what they want.
2. To give them an opportunity to talk about the ways other people get caught in their games.
3. To provide an opportunity for children to practice ways of communicating their needs and feelings directly.

DIRECTIONS: Use only after you have spent time on *GAMES PARENTS PLAY* so that they understand what these games are and how it feels to be "caught" in these games. They have also had an opportunity to practice using "I" messages, as a way of communicating their needs directly.

Evoke from the children the "games" they play with their parents in order to get what they want, such as:

1. "If you love me, I'll be on your side."
2. "Give me what I want and I'll love."
3. "But daddy says I can."
4. "If you marry him/her I won't live with/visit you anymore."
5. "Dad, mom won't let me . . ."

Make a list of the responses. Then ask the children to choose one of the situations. Younger children can use their puppets to portray the situation. Older children can use role playing. Help them see the ways they are manipulating and hurting not only their parents but themselves.

Have the situations reenacted again in such a way that the children communicate directly with the parents what they are feeling and the parents giving honest responses to how they are feeling.

WHAT WOULD I DO?

MATERIALS NEEDED: *WHAT WOULD I DO?* handout

PURPOSE: Teens find themselves in situations which leave them confused and not knowing how to react. In addressing these issues they can begin to find some ways of dealing with their response to the situations as well as with their feelings about them.

DIRECTIONS: Use the situations listed on the *WHAT WOULD I DO?* handout. Identify the situation and then ask for a direct response from the group in arriving at their feelings and a healthy response to the situation.

OR

Divide the students into groups. Give each group one or more situations for them to role play. After presenting their role playing to the entire group, enter into a discussion about what was going on, what various characters were feeling, and their reaction to the way the actors dealt with the problem.

WHAT WOULD I DO?

What would *you* do and how would *you* feel if:

1. Your father (mother) has a new girlfriend (boyfriend) and suddenly his (her) dating behavior seems a lot like your own?

2. Your mom (dad) tells you she (he) is going to get married again and you don't like the new person? You do like the new person?

3. Mom (dad) is dating, but the rules about sex are not the same for her (him) as they are for you?

4. You go to the wedding of a good friend or relative and both of your parents are present?

5. You see your mom (dad) happy with her (his) new boyfriend (girlfriend), but your dad (mom) is at home feeling sad and lonely?

6. You think about the time in the future when you will be married and have children?

7. You think about the mistakes you saw your parents make in their relationship? You think about the way they each must feel? You try to understand whose fault it was?

8. You see your dad (mom) going to mass on Sundays, even though he (she) left your mom (dad) for another woman (man)?

9. You think about how your mom (dad) has changed since the divorce? You think about your mom (dad) as a parent since the divorce?

10. Dad's new girlfriend asks you to come to her house for a visit? Mom's new boyfriend asks you to come to his house for a visit?

WHEN I STOP TO THINK

MATERIALS NEEDED: *WHEN I STOP TO THINK* handout, pencils, personal notebooks or additional paper

PURPOSE: Adolescents have many concerns about their present situation as well as about the future. This exercise is designed to help them focus directly on a number of issues they need to explore. It is a way of helping them sort out much of the confusion they feel as a teenager, complicated by divorce.

DIRECTIONS: Give each student a copy of the handout, *WHEN I STOP TO THINK*. Have them go to a quiet place to write. Provide sufficient time for them to respond to each question either on another paper or in their personal notebook.

When the group has finished writing, open the discussion with something like:

You have had time to respond to a variety of issues which touch your life. Mark the three which are of the greatest concern to you.

Invite response from the group. This material can be used for several sessions.

WHEN I STOP TO THINK

Complete the following thoughts:

1. At this moment, the most important thing in the world to me is _____
   _____

2. Since my parents' divorce, I _____
   _____

3. Urgent needs I have are _____
   _____

4. The hardest thing about my family situation now is_____
   _____

5. My greatest source of strength is_____
   _____

6. My mother is _____
   _____

7. Emotionally, I feel _____
   _____

8. My father is _____
   _____

9. For the future, I would like to _____
   _____

10. The divorce experience helped me to_____
    _____

11. If I get married _____

_____

12. Men are _____

_____

13. Women are _____

_____

14. God_____

_____

15. To forgive, I _____

_____

16. I wish my mother_____

_____

17. I wish my father_____

_____

18. I am most afraid of_____

_____

19. The thing I just can't get over is _____

_____

20. I don't understand _____

_____

THE CATHOLIC CHURCH AND DIVORCE

MATERIALS NEEDED: THE CATHOLIC CHURCH AND DIVORCE fact sheet

PURPOSE: To provide information and the opportunity to provide for open discussion on church issues. There is a great deal of misunderstanding about the position of the Catholic Church and divorce.

DIRECTIONS: Provide students with the fact sheet which can be used as a guide to explore their questions in regard to the church and divorce. Be prepared for other questions that the students may ask. If you do not know the answer either, don't hesitate to tell them so and offer to have the information for them at another session.

This may be a good time to invite a priest or someone knowledgeable about church law to meet with the teens. It is important that they try to understand the struggle of the church to uphold its teaching on the permanence of marriage while at the same time reaching out with compassion to those whose marriages have not survived.

THE CATHOLIC CHURCH AND DIVORCE FACT SHEET

1. The Catholic Church upholds its teaching on the permanence of marriage and therefore does not recognize divorce.

2. Because the church does not recognize divorce, the divorced person continues to be a fully participating member of the church and free to receive the sacraments.

3. The Catholic Church does recognize that people get a civil divorce for a variety of reasons and that this can be a most painful experience for those involved.

4. The church reaches out with care and compassion to those who are separated and divorced in an effort to help them deal with their pain, to rebuild their lives, to remain a part of the church and to preserve their relationship with God.

5. To marry again after a divorce a person must prove that the first marriage was not a valid sacramental marriage.

6. Some marriages are invalid because the couple did not follow the form required by the Catholic Church, i.e. married by a justice of the peace. This is called a lack of form.

7. Many marriages have received a church annulment. This means that the marriage is not binding until death as far as the church is concerned.

8. When an annulment is granted by the tribunal (a group of church-lawyers within the diocese) the marriage is declared annulled or non-sacramental.

9. This in no way affects the civil validity of the marriage or the legitimacy of children.

10. To obtain an annulment, a divorced person is asked:
    a. to have a legal, civil divorce if he/she is a U.S. citizen
    b. to answer questions
    c. to have two witnesses
    d. to consider paying a small fee to the tribunal (no one is turned away because of an inability to pay)

11. It can take ten or more months to obtain an annulment in the Catholic Church. It all depends on the details of the case and the cooperation of those answering the questions.

12. The Catholic Church recognizes the marriage of two Protestants by a minister as a sacramental union because they are two believers in Jesus. Therefore, a divorced Protestant may need to obtain an annulment to be married in the Catholic Church.

13. The Catholic Church acts with compassion toward its separated/divorced members. Some priests, deacons and lay persons are specially trained to help them to go through the annulment process. Many dioceses have special programs designed to assist adults and children in dealing with their loss.

107

ISSUES

Use *GAMES PARENTS PLAY* handout as you write in your journal this week.

1. Look over the examples given on *GAMES PARENTS PLAY*. Choose those which are similar to your experience. Describe your experience and what you could do to make it more positive.

2. Pretend you are talking to your mother and/or your dad about getting caught between them in their anger toward one another. What would you like to tell them about how you feel? What needs to change?

3. Choose a particular situation with which you have difficulty dealing. Carry on a conversation with the person involved in such a way that you communicate your difficulty to them. Listening to their response, bring the situation to a satisfactory conclusion.

4. Write a letter to an imaginary boy or girl who has asked your advice in dealing with a particular "parent" issue.

5. To help you come in touch with how you are feeling, complete the following phrase: "When you (talk negatively about dad), I feel (disloyal) because (I love both you and dad).

6. It is easy to see the "games" your parents play because you are the one who gets caught in them. What games do you play? Some examples are:
   "Love me more if I side with you."
   "Do this for me and I'll love you."
   "But daddy lets me do it."
   "If you marry him/her I won't live with/visit you anymore."
   "Dad, mom won't let me . . ."

After you have added to this list, choose one or two. Write about how you feel, and why you need to play the game in order to manipulate your parent(s). Write some options you have for other kinds of behavior or ways to express more directly and honestly what you *really* need.

In your journal carry on a conversation with your mom or your dad in which you let them know how much they are hurt when you "play games" to get what you want or to control them.

CLOSURE

- To build self-esteem
- To set some personal goals
- To put closure on the SUNRISE group experience

Closure is like a rite of passage. Children need to say goodbye to the family they used to be and to what can never be for them so that they can move on with their life. This is what they have been doing throughout the SUNRISE sessions. Now it is time to put closure on their SUNRISE experience.

These weeks spent together have created significant bonds for the children. They often find it difficult to leave a group which has provided such warmth, understanding and security.

This section provides ways for the children to plan for their life without the SUNRISE group, to look back on their time together and to say goodbye to the group.

Qualities: In Session I children were encouraged to draw a self portrait and to write descriptive words under their picture. Now is the time for them to focus on their growth over these weeks together. This can be done by drawing a new self portrait with new descriptive words or by talking about what has been learned and how SUNRISE has helped each child.

It is important for them to leave the group feeling good about themselves.

Goals: In Session I children expressed some goals they wanted to accomplish. Refer to these goals to see what was accomplished. Add to it insights gained, feelings and issues faced and anything else they want to add to their list of accomplishments.

You might find it appropriate to draw and/or talk about goals children want to accomplish in the weeks ahead. These may concern family, relationships, school achievements or involvement in other types of groups or activities.

Follow-Up: This section contains questions for children to take home and ask their parents. There are also some questions for parents to ask in order to open dialogue with their children. It is hoped that by this time children have gained the skills and confidence to communicate honestly and openly with their parents.

HOW I HAVE CHANGED

MATERIALS NEEDED: Drawing paper or *HOW I HAVE CHANGED* handout, pencils, colored pencils, crayons or magic markers

PURPOSE: The children have drawn their self portrait early in the SUNRISE session and used words to describe themselves. This is a repeat of that same exercise. However, at this time it is hoped that the children have grown and have a much better image of themselves so that it will be a revelation to them when they compare the two projects. This is one way that their self-esteem can be enhanced.

DIRECTIONS: Give each child a piece of drawing paper or the *HOW I HAVE CHANGED* handout, providing the necessary art supplies.

Draw a picture of yourself. When you have finished, write on the paper words which describe you now such as friendly, angry, tough guy, pretty caring, hopeful, etc.

Even if their feelings seem to be negative, this can be a positive outgrowth of the SUNRISE experience. The group might have enabled the children to be more realistic and honest about their feelings and offered healthy ways of expressing them.

When they have completed their work, give them the picture they drew at the beginning of the SUNRISE session. Lead them into sharing the difference between the two.

- *As you look at both pictures, what do you notice is different?*

- *How have the words changed which you used to describe yourself?*

- *How have you changed since you began SUNRISE?*
  . . . in your attitude
  . . . in your behavior
  . . . in your relationship with your parent(s)
  . . . in your relationship with your brothers/sisters
  . . . in your relationship with your friends
  . . . in your school work
  . . . in your feelings about yourself

111

HOW I HAVE CHANGED

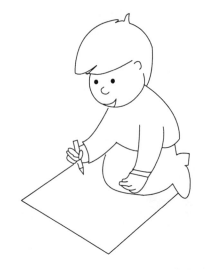

WORDS WHICH DESCRIBE ME

MATERIALS NEEDED: *WORDS WHICH DESCRIBE ME* handout for each child, pencils, colored paper (8 1/2 x 11" suggested), straight pins, magic markers of various colors

PURPOSE: Each child in the group has experienced a great deal of pain as a result of his or her parents' divorce. Part of the consequence of this pain is a sense of low self-esteem.

During the weeks in SUNRISE it is hoped that the children have begun to feel better about themselves. This exercise is a visible way that they can affirm in themselves and in one another the gifts that they see.

DIRECTIONS: Talk to the children about how each of them is unique since God made them just as they are. God gave them special gifts. You can mention a few.

Give each child the handout and a pencil. Ask the children to check those qualities which best describe them. There is also space for the children to add to the list.

After giving them time to complete the handout, have them all sit in a circle. Give them each a blank piece of paper and a pin. Have them turn to the person on their right and pin the paper on that person's back. Then give them each a magic marker. Have them go around to each person and write one gift that they see in that person.

When they have completed this, have the children return to the circle. Take some time for each child to share with the group the qualities he/she checked on the list. You may want to have them give reasons for this choice. Then have them take the list from their back and see what the other children have written about them.

This is a sensitive time, so it needs to be handled with care. However, if appropriate, you may wish to ask the children to give reasons why they chose particular qualities for one another.

WORDS WHICH DESCRIBE ME

_____ CHEERFUL

_____ FRIENDLY

_____ KIND

_____ ENTHUSIASTIC

_____ QUIET

_____ POLITE

_____ JOYFUL

_____ HAPPY

_____ RESERVED

_____ STUDIOUS

_____ INTERESTING

_____ HONEST

_____ HELPFUL

_____ OPTIMISTIC

_____ PATIENT

_____ OUTGOING

_____ SERIOUS

_____ FUN-LOVING

_____ GOOD LISTENER

_____ ACCEPTING OF OTHERS

_____ CONSIDERATE

_____

_____

_____

WHAT I'VE DONE FOR MYSELF

MATERIALS NEEDED: Goals which were set in "What I Want for Myself" in Section I, crayons/magic markers

PURPOSE: By recalling the goals set at the first session as well as focusing on other insights gained during the following weeks, children can feel some sense of accomplishment as they put closure on their time in the support group.

DIRECTIONS: Return to the children the paper on which they wrote their original goals. Give them time to decorate this paper and add to it any additional insights they may have gained during the previous weeks. This can be done in words or in pictures.

You might also wish to have the children share whatever they wish after they have completed their project. Some may want to share their goals and how they feel about achieving or not achieving them. Some of the goals might be more ongoing and take a longer period of time to achieve. They may need to talk about this.

It is also a good time to focus on other areas which the children felt were helpful throughout the sessions.

DO YOU NEED TO KNOW?

MATERIALS NEEDED: *DO YOU NEED TO KNOW?* handout for each child

PURPOSE: During these weeks together children have talked about their feelings and about situations in which they find themselves as a result of their parents' divorce. They might still have some questions they need to ask their parents.

DIRECTIONS: Before using these questions, communicate with the parents so that they will be prepared for the questions their children will ask. You might want to send them a copy of the questions with a summary of the things done in the SUNRISE group.

Give each child a copy of the questions with instructions similar to these:

We have shared a great deal during these weeks. Some of you have also talked to at least one of your parents about the effect their divorce has had on you.

I'm now giving you some specific questions. Read them over. If there are questions you want answered, find a time in which your mother or your dad can sit down with you without being disturbed. Tell them you'd like to ask them some questions about the divorce.

Remember, your mother and dad were also hurt by the divorce so you need to communicate your love to them at the same time you are asking questions which might be difficult to ask and possibly more difficult for your parent to answer.

About a week before using this handout with the children, mail the questions to their parent(s) with a letter explaining that their children will be approaching them with these questions. In this letter you might want to include *QUESTIONS FOR PARENTS TO ASK CHILDREN.*

DO YOU NEED TO KNOW?

1. Why did you get a divorce?

2. Why do you yell so much?

3. Why did you (dad/mom) have to move far away?

4. Do you like living without a husband/wife?

5. Do you like living alone?

6. How would it feel to get a new husband/wife?

7. How does it feel to get a divorce?

8. Why did you start fighting?

9. Why did you make me sad by getting a divorce?

10. Was it my fault that you got a divorce?

11. Would you like to live with dad/mom again?

12. How would you feel if you got married again and then got divorced again?

13. Why do you compete with each other to see who is more generous to me?

14. Why do you still fight so much? Do you think you will ever stop?

15. What do you think it would be like if you were still together?

16. Why do the mothers usually get the kids?

17. Why are you so angry with dad/mom all the time?

18. Why do you take your anger out on me?

19. Why can't you two get together now and be friends?

20. Why did you change so much after the divorce?

21. If you get married again, will you have more kids?

22. If you loved each other when you got married, why don't you love each other now?

23. Will you leave me too?

QUESTIONS FOR PARENTS TO ASK CHILDREN

MATERIALS NEEDED: *QUESTIONS FOR PARENTS TO ASK CHILDREN* handout

PURPOSE: These questions are designed for parents as guides for them to begin talking about issues with their children which have not been addressed previously in order to increase the communication between parent and child as well as to offer children the opportunity to talk more directly about what they are feeling and thinking.

DIRECTIONS: The handout is merely a guide for the parent(s). Therefore, to be most effective the questions are not read to the child. Rather, in a quiet and uninterrupted setting, the parent can informally begin surfacing these and similar questions with the child/children.

It may be more beneficial, if there is more than one child, to plan a special time with each one individually. In this way they can have some special time with the parent as well as be free from the influence of other children.

At the end of the SUNRISE program, mail a copy of *QUESTIONS FOR PARENTS TO ASK CHILDREN* with a note similar to the following:

Dear Parent,

Your child/children has/have now completed the SUNRISE program. We hope that it has been a positive experience for them.

We encourage you to continue what has begun here through open dialogue. To facilitate this sharing between you and your child, I am enclosing a copy of some questions which you can use to explore those issues which might still be unresolved.

We suggest that you study the questions yourself, adding others according to your situation. Keeping these questions in mind, set aside a special time with your child which will be quiet and uninterrupted. If you have more than one child, you may find it beneficial to spend time with each one individually.

Let me know if you have any further questions.

QUESTIONS FOR PARENTS TO ASK CHILDREN

1. Why don't you write or call your father/mother?

2. Why do you get angry at me after visiting your father/mother?

3. Why are you so angry all the time?

4. How would you feel if I got married again? What about dad/mom?

5. Why do you take advantage of me? Why are you always testing me?

6. Do you really understand why we got a divorce? What would you like to know?

7. Why do you fight so much?

8. Are you happy living with me?

9. Why don't you talk with me more often?

10. How did you feel when dad/mom left? How do you feel about him/her now?

11. How do you feel about me dating? What about dad/mom?

12. Do you feel the kids in school treat you differently because your parents are divorced?

ENDING

1. Write about your feelings as you leave the SUNRISE group.

2. List the names of each person in your SUNRISE group. Next to each one write how they have helped you during your weeks together. Include what you hope for them as they move out of the group. Share this in your SUNRISE group if you feel comfortable doing so.

3. Write a letter to yourself telling what you like about yourself.

4. What are the main things you have learned—about yourself, about coping with your parents' divorce or about understanding the situation—during your time in SUNRISE.

5. Develop a specific plan for yourself in continuing to improve in those areas which have caused you the most difficulties.

   . . . relationship with your mother

   . . . relationship with your father

   . . . relationship with brothers/sisters

   . . . relationships in school

   . . . developing a hobby

   . . . any others

6. Reflecting on your own experience, how can you reach out to others whose parents are separated or divorced?

PRAYER AND RITUAL

- To center SUNRISE in an experience of God
- To provide ways of relating to God
- To help children discover God in their pain
- To offer opportunities for spiritual healing

Ritual is a way of expressing an experience at a deeper level. In this section you will find ways to ritualize forgiveness and closure. If the SUNRISE group has a religious orientation, it also provides an excellent opportunity for children to tap into their spiritual roots.

Prayer: Under "Prayer" you will find some sample prayers. Use these or develop your own. Have the children take turns making up their own prayer. The important thing is that children realize that God is there with them always no matter what they do or say, that they are loved by God, and that they can talk to God in their own way about what is happening in their lives.

Notice that the SUNRISE prayers do not address God as male or female. Most children have learned to address God as Father. However, if their experience of "father" is negative, they will not be able to relate positively to a Father-God. Allow them to develop their own images and to address God in any way they wish.

Not only are the SUNRISE prayers modeling an image of God, they are also expressing some aspects that the children need to learn if they are to deal adequately with their parents' divorce, i.e. the divorce is not their fault, it's O.K. not to want to spend a whole weekend with the non-custodial parent, there are ways to tell their parents how they feel, feelings are nei-

ther good nor bad, etc. The prayers help them realize that they can say anything to God and still be accepted and loved.

Prayer can also be a way for children to cope with all the confusion around them. When there seems to be no one around who understands, it helps to be able to talk to God.

It is recommended that you begin each session with a simple introductory prayer such as: "God, you are with us always. Help us to remember your love and care for us as we begin our SUNRISE group today." The longer prayers can be said at the end of each session, using the concepts, concerns or issues that were expressed during their time together.

Another way to end the group is to make a circle. If children are comfortable holding hands, have them do so. Invite them to pray for anyone or anything they wish. Encourage them to pray for their parents. You might want to start this circle prayer by saying something like: "God, please heal my son who is sick today."

Forgiveness: When we feel hurt by someone, it is difficult to forgive, especially for children. However, forgiveness and acceptance of the limitations of others is a part of the healing process. Under "Forgiveness" you will find sample forgiveness rituals. Adapt them to the age and experience of the children in your group. Plan a forgiveness ritual about three-fourths of the way through the SUNRISE sessions.

Closure: As a concluding SUNRISE session, it is recommended that a group or a family prayer experience be provided. In the "Closure" section several samples are given. However, use your own creativity to develop what would be most appropriate for your group.

PRAYERS FOR YOUNG CHILDREN

Dear Jesus,
please let me be
part of your Holy Family. Amen.

Jesus,
help me to pray,
help me to play,
help me to do what you say. Amen.

O my God,
please help me to know
that you will take care of mom/dad
wherever they go. Amen.

Dearest Jesus,
your family lost you once.
I know how they felt.
My dad/mom is gone.
Help me to go on. Amen

Mother Mary, love me.
Saint Joseph, protect me.
Brother Jesus, show me the way. Amen.

HELLO, GOD

LET'S BEGIN

Hello, God. Here I am in the SUNRISE group. I don't want to be here. I feel strange. But you know, as I look around, I realize that I'm not the only kid whose parents are divorced. Maybe it won't be so bad after all.

Hello, God. I've met some nice friends. Their parents are divorced, too. It makes me feel better to know I'm not the only one. Thanks, God, for SUNRISE and new friends.

Hello, God. Sometimes I find it really hard to come to SUNRISE, but I know it's important for me to be here. I want to feel good about myself. I want to learn how to cope with my parents' divorce. Help me to have the courage to stick with my SUNRISE group no matter how I feel.

FAMILY

Hello, God. I just don't understand what's happening in my family. Dad doesn't live with us anymore and I miss him so much. I want mom and dad to be together again, but I know I can't make that happen. Please, God, take care of mom and dad for me.

Hello, God. There have been so many changes in my life lately. It's really hard. Sometimes I'm even afraid of what will happen next. I know you are with me no matter what happens. Just hold my hand a little tighter, please!

GRIEF PROCESS

Hello, God. Sometimes I feel like I'm on a roller coaster. One day I am sad and lonely, the next day I feel like things are going smoothly and I feel good. Then I start wishing that this divorce had never happened and I get angry. I know these up and down feelings are normal. I guess I just need to tell you now and then how I feel because I know you're always here to listen.

Hello, God. I keep telling myself that mom will soon come back home to live with us and everything will be like it always was. But deep down I know that won't happen. It hurts so much to face the truth. Help me, God. Take my hand and walk with me.

FEELINGS

Hello, God. I love feeling good. It feels so good to laugh, to look forward to something, to receive a warm hug. But there are some feelings that don't feel so good. I don't like being sad. I don't like so many other feelings for which I don't even have words. Help me to know that all these feelings—good and bad—are O.K. and that I'm O.K. too.

Hello, God. It seems like I've been so angry lately. I say and do things that hurt other people. I don't really know why I act this way. Help me to find ways to use my "angry energy" in ways that will make me feel good about myself, my family and my friends.

Hello, God. Sometimes I feel so guilty about my parents' divorce. They keep telling me that it wasn't my fault, but somehow, deep inside, I'm not so sure. Help me, God, to realize that it really wasn't my fault and to let go of my guilty feelings.

ISSUES

Hello, God. You know I don't like leaving home each weekend to see dad. I love him and want to be with him, but I want to be with my friends, too. Help me to talk to dad about how I feel. Help us to figure out a way to spend time together and still have time with my friends.

Hello, God. So often I feel forced to take sides with one of my parents. I know they don't get along, but I love both of them. Help me, God, to tell them each how much I care, but that I just don't want to get caught in the middle. This will be hard. Help me to figure out what to say and to choose the right time to say it. Thanks, God.

SELF-ESTEEM

Hello, God. I am so glad to be *me*. Sometimes I think I'm too fat or too short or too silly. But you love me just the way I am. And you know, God, I want to thank you for making me so special. There is no one else just like me!

THE FORGIVENESS KNOT

MATERIALS NEEDED: One-fourth inch cording from a fabric or craft shop cut in lengths of about twelve inches for each child, scissors

PURPOSE: This exercise is helpful for children who have difficulty forgiving one or both parents. It gives them a tangible experience of their pain and the consequences of non-forgiveness. It also serves as a vehicle for dialogue and movement toward forgiveness.

DIRECTIONS: Give each child a piece of cord. Open this guided imagery with a brief introduction similar to the following:

Sometimes it is difficult to forgive our parents for their decision to divorce. Let the cord represent the relationship between you and one or both of your parents whom you have difficulty forgiving. When we don't forgive, we usually behave in a way that puts distance between us and the other person. Cut your cord in half. This represents the broken or strained relationship. One of these pieces represents you. Tie a knot at the end of your half. Now we are going to use our imagination.

Using some soft background music, lead the children in a guided imagery similar to the following:

In each hand hold a piece of the cord. Get into a comfortable position. Close your eyes. Take a deep, deep breath through your nose. Exhale through your mouth. Do this several times. Imagine the air going into your body and back out again.

Allow several minutes for the children to do this deep breathing.

Place the unknotted cord on your lap. Carefully slide your hand along the cord with the knot. Notice how smooth it is until you come to the knot. Hold the knot in your hand. Roll it around with your fingers so you can feel every part of it. Imagine the knot as your behavior which creates an invisible wall between you and your parent or parents. We sometimes build walls to protect ourselves from being hurt again. However, when we do this, we usually create even more pain for ourselves.

Think of some times that your stomach felt like this knot. Can you remember the situation? Try to remember how you felt. Perhaps you were angry or afraid or lonely.

Having your parents divorced isn't easy. Many things have changed, and so you build up resentment which can be like weights holding you down. It's hard to forgive. But as long as you have that knot at the end of the cord, the two pieces can't reconnect. As long as you refuse to forgive, you cannot build a relationship with those you love. Forgiveness is a decision.

With your eyes still closed, untie the knot at the end of the cord. Now both cords are smooth, so tie them together. The relationship can once again be restored. What do you need to change in order to knock down that invisible wall between you and your parent or parents? What do you need to say to acknowledge your forgiveness? What do you need from your mom—from your dad?

Again slide your hand along the cord. The knot is there, but in a different way. The knot is now connecting the two cords. The cords that were two are now one. A knot is still there because we can't change what happened, but it has changed. We have learned something and we try not to let the pain separate us from those we love. We don't let it cut off our relationship. We can work around the knot and find new ways to bridge the relationship. The relationship doesn't have to end.

Imagine you are with that parent you have had difficulty forgiving. Think of what you would say to him or her after you have made the decision to forgive.

Allow sufficient time for this internal conversation to take place.

Now slowly come back in your imagination to this room and slowly open your eyes.

Give children a bit of time to move out of the guided imagery.

This process can be concluded with a short prayer, or it can be an opportunity for the children to talk about their willingness or unwillingness to forgive.

Some children may be so angry or in such awkward and difficult situations with one or both parents that it is not possible for them to forgive at this time. Let them know that this is all right. Forgiveness takes time. However, remind them of the knot that will always be there separating them unless they make the decision to untie it.

Our unwillingness to forgive does not necessarily hurt the other person. It hurts us!

A SUNRISE FORGIVENESS

MATERIALS NEEDED: A large black circle cut from construction paper, two yellow circles the same size cut in wedges to equal the number of children in the group

PURPOSE: To help children realize that when they refuse to forgive, their behavior is affected.

To offer optional ways of behaving which express their forgiveness toward those they love.

DIRECTIONS: This is a ritual which can be done together with all the children of various age groups in the SUNRISE program.

Show the large black circle to the children. Say something like the following:

Your behavior toward others usually lets them know your willingness or your unwillingness to forgive them for something they have said or done. People usually know when you refuse to forgive them. You might not speak to them or you might wear a long face or say and do some mean things to them. You are not happy and the other person doesn't enjoy being around you when you act like this. It is like having a dark cloud hanging over you so you can't see the sun shining. It is like this big black circle.

Take some time for the children to talk about their struggle to forgive—what they say and do to hurt others when they are hurting themselves and how they feel when they are unable to forgive. Can they identify with the dark cloud?

Then continue, giving each child a yellow wedge:

But we're going to make the sun shine again. Think of some loving, generous, kind things you can do or say to show that you forgive someone, like "I'm sorry"—ways that will bring the SUNRISE back into your life.

Have the children share their ideas. As they do, ask them to come forward and begin filling in the black circle with their yellow wedge. When the circle is completely covered, the remaining pieces can be placed around the outside of the circle like rays of the sun. Relate this to SUNRISE. The purpose of SUNRISE is to remove the darkness so that the sun can shine again in their lives.

End this session with a group prayer circle. Invite the children to ask God to help them to forgive and to change any behavior that might hurt someone else.

FROM DARKNESS TO LIGHT

MATERIALS NEEDED: Pictures from "My Feelings in Color" from Section III, black or dark colored crayon, paper clips

PURPOSE: To give children a visual experience of how they have let go and changed during their weeks in SUNRISE.

To take a look at what/whom they have forgiven or what/whom they want to forgive.

DIRECTIONS: Have the children look in their folder or bag to find the feelings they colored from "My Feelings in Color." If you have saved them, return them to each child.

Tell the children to choose one of the more colorful drawings. Give the following directions:

Think about how you have changed since you drew these pictures. Each of them is a memory of something painful. Take one which expresses a feeling about a situation which is now past and those involved are forgiven or at least you want to forgive them.

Using a dark colored crayon (black, purple, dark blue), color over your entire picture. Press hard so only the dark color shows.

Allow time for them to do this.

Help the children talk about times when they were so confused and hurt that they didn't know what to do or to say. It was almost like being in the dark—like their pictures.

Then say to them:

You have come through some pretty dark times, but you have grown and changed. Some positive things have happened since you started in SUNRISE. Some of you have discovered the change because you have been willing to forgive.

Think of a symbol which expresses the life and growth you feel now. Then take a paper clip and scratch off the dark color in the form of

your new symbol—a sunrise, a happy face, a butterfly or whatever expresses what you are feeling now. The light color from the original will show through.

Have the children talk about their new feeling and how important it is to allow themselves to feel the happy as well as the sad feelings.

THE BENT-OVER WOMAN

MATERIALS NEEDED: Copy of song (optional), a person dressed in old shabby clothes, basket or box, paper, pencil, background music

PURPOSE: To provide a ritualized expression of closure for the SUNRISE group.

To enable children to see how their positive response to others can be healing.

DIRECTIONS: It is suggested that you bring together all the children from the various SUNRISE age groups. If at all possible, invite their parents—both parents. Inform the parents that this has been a most significant time for their children. Ask them if they could both be present for this closing service.

If both parents come, be sensitive to the fact that this might be an anxious and strained time for them. Help to make them feel as comfortable as possible.

The following is a ritual which you can use.

SONG:

WELCOME:

OPENING PRAYER: *All-powerful God, you call us through baptism to freedom and new life. Your Son Jesus has touched us and has shown the way to wholeness. Send your Holy Spirit now to be our helper and guide. Give us wisdom and understanding, courage and right judgment, knowledge and reverence. Fill us with the spirit of wonder and awe in your presence with us daily. We ask this in Jesus' name. Amen.*

SCRIPTURE/ REFLECTION: Tell the story of the bent-over woman from Luke 13:10-17. As the story is being told, have another adult play the part of this woman. She is dressed in shabby clothes, carries a cane, has gnarled hands and is extremely bent. She walks around the room with an expression of anger, pain and confusion. She feels her way because she is blind.

After the story is told, pause to allow the observers to just sit and watch this woman in her pain. Then ask the children how they think this woman must feel.

When they run out of ideas, have the woman add some thoughts of her own such as: "My back hurts. I can't see where I'm going. It's difficult to hear. I find it hard to breathe. My hands are crippled and ache constantly. People seem to avoid me."

Then ask the children:

What can you do to ease her pain?

One might say to give her a hug. Tell that child to go to the woman and give her a hug. Receiving the hug, the old woman begins to stand a bit taller. Another child might suggest a kind greeting. Invite each child to go up to the old woman and express his or her greeting, prayer or gesture. Each time the woman is healed more fully until she is standing straight, healed of all her ailments.

When this healing ritual is completed, have each family gather together. Give them paper and pencil. Ask them to write the struggles that cause the various family members to feel bent-over like this woman. Ask them also to write their strengths as individuals and as families.

After they have had time to write and then share with their family, invite each family to come forward and drop their paper into a basket or box which is being held by the bent-over woman now healed. (Play background music during the offering.)

PRAYER OVER
THE OFFERINGS:

Spirit of God, breathe into our families new life. Make us strong in those areas in which we are weak. Help us to see the strengths we have as a family. Help us to love one another unselfishly and find ways to show our love. With your help we can do this through Jesus. Amen.

PETITIONS:

*For the people throughout the world who are fighting, that they may forgive one another and live in peace, we pray to the Lord.
. . . Lord, heal us.*

For our priests, bishops and all clergy, that they may continue to minister to all those who are in need, we pray to the Lord.
. . . Lord heal us.

For all our families who are angry and hurting, we pray to the Lord.
. . . Lord heal us.

For each of us here, that we may let go of our feelings of guilt, rejection and anger so that we can be free to forgive those who have hurt us, we pray to the Lord.
. . . Lord heal us.

For the continued happiness we experience through SUNRISE, we pray to the Lord.
. . . Lord heal us.

OUR FATHER:

GREETING OF PEACE: Invite family members to embrace one another and in some way express their concern, love, forgiveness (whatever seems appropriate).

WORD OF THANKS: Acknowledge the parents and communicate to them the importance of their presence and their participation in this closing ritual.

CLOSING PRAYER: *God our creator and Jesus our brother, you are the way, the truth and the life. You promise that after the darkness of each night, the sun will rise. We pray that each of us will remember your promise and how we have moved through darkness to new life in SUNRISE. Today we say goodbye to SUNRISE, but may we never forget what we have learned. Give us a deep faith, peace and the ability to trust again. We ask this in Jesus' name. Amen.*

SONG:

CELEBRATION: Conclude with refreshments.

THE SUNRISE GIFT

MATERIALS NEEDED: Letters, symbols, verses which the leader has collected throughout SUNRISE, paper or journal, pencils, background music

PURPOSE: To give children a sense of what they have accomplished through their participation in SUNRISE.

To have children leave SUNRISE with positive feelings about themselves.

To see SUNRISE as a gift to themselves.

DIRECTIONS: *Remote Preparation*

At the beginning of the SUNRISE program prepare a bag for each child with his or her name printed on it. At the end of each session write a note, a scripture passage, a piece of poetry or a symbol which expresses something significant about the child during that session. You might want to refer to the child's willingness to face the pain, to reach out to others in the group, to express his or her feelings, etc.

You could also extend an invitation to teachers and parents to contribute to the "Gift Bag." If not every week, at least they could add something for this closing ritual. Staple the bags shut before giving them to the children.

During the Session

Have the children get into a comfortable position. They might want to stretch out on the floor or go outside. You are going to take them through a guided imagery. While you are doing this, have someone else present who can place the "Gift Bag" next to each child so that when the children open their eyes, they will find it. Give the following instructions:

Get into a comfortable position. I'm going to take you on an imaginary trip. Close your eyes and breathe deeply. Breathe in through your nose. Let the air move all through your body. Then exhale through your mouth. Do this several times.

Allow some time for them to do this breathing exercise. Then read the following guided imagery slowly, pausing to allow children time to move through the experience.

Imagine yourself walking down a country road. The sun is shining and there is a refreshing breeze. It is a beautiful day. Gradually the road becomes a path which takes you into a woods. You are surrounded by trees of every size and shape. You look around and see a rabbit dart behind a tree. A little further you see a deer peering at you from a distance. As you get closer, it turns and runs. You run after it until you come to a clearing. Before you is a beautiful meadow filled with wild flowers. You stop to pick a few.

Suddenly you are aware of a house ahead of you. You realize that this house belongs to you. What does it look like?

You approach the house, open the door and walk inside, closing the door behind you. What is it like? What do you do when you get inside? How do you feel? This is your house. You are comfortable here.

Spend some time here. What do you do?

Allow time for children to answer these questions to themselves and to explore their house.

You want someone to join you in your house—your mom, your dad, Jesus, someone you trust. Invite your guest to join you. Sit down and talk. What do you say? What do they say to you?

Now your guest must leave. You say goodbye knowing that you can invite them back at any time.

Now you must leave too. You get up, open the door, walk out and close the door behind you. You realize that this is your special place—a place where you are safe, a place where you can go at anytime. You walk across the meadow, down the path through the woods. You are now back on the country road.

As you walk along, slowly open your eyes and see that you are back here.

Allow time for children to get reoriented. When they open their eyes, they will see the "Gift Bag." Say to them:

Each of you has a "Gift Bag." They have been specially prepared for you. Take it, your journal or paper and pencil to an area where you can have some private space. Open the bags and take out the treasures you find. When you are finished, write about what you are feeling.

Allow time for the children to do this. When they seem ready, bring them together again. Ask them to share anything they wish about the guided imagery or the contents from the "Gift Bag." It is all right if they don't want to share.

Remind them that this is the last SUNRISE session, so it is important to say goodbye. Help them to talk about the gift that SUNRISE has been to them and the gift they have been to one another.

FACILITATING THE SUNRISE GROUP

Before we work with children, let's take a look at ourselves. In order that we may effectively work with other people and particularly people with special needs, it is important to make sure that we are in touch with our own special needs. Working with the group is a great opportunity for us to make sure we know what's going on inside us. Extending ourselves for others helps in our own growth process.

1. Reflecting on our own family background, what did we learn from our parents? What were we taught to feel about ourselves? What feelings are accepted or not accepted? How have we managed to meet our own needs since we left the original family?

2. It's a good idea to assess our own present family system. How are our own relationships with our children, friends, spouse? Is there dysfunction in our own home?

3. What is our personal experience with divorce? Are we thinking of facilitating a group because we want to extend to others what we have gained through our own pain and struggle? Are we reaching out to help heal our own pain? How can the experience of facilitating a group assist us in our own growth process?

4. What might be some other motivations for working with a group? Do we need to feel needed? Are we still fresh in pain and grief?

5. Can we accept ourselves as we are now? Do we love ourselves despite our many shortcomings? Can we do enough to please ourselves? Are we trying to please others?

6. Do we believe in the process of healing which follows crisis, trauma, grief and loss? Have we seen it worked through before, either in our own life or the life of someone else?

7. Are we able to cope with our own anger? Do we accept our angry self? How do we handle angry feelings? What people or situations push our buttons? Do we have a short fuse?

8. Are we able to accept responsibility for our own personal problems or do we feel that our misfortunes are the fault of someone else?

9. Can we remain sufficiently objective in the face of the pain, anger, and grief of a child to be able to remain supportive for that child? Do we sometimes get pulled into the child's emotionality?

10. Do we feel warmly toward children most of the time?

11. Do we possess some personal and/or professional knowledge about human behavior?

12. Are we patient by nature? Is it hard for us to stand by and watch someone struggle through a process? Is it our tendency to jump in and try to solve the problems of others?

13. Can we resist rescuing a child who is struggling through the grief process? Can we remain supportive, but sufficiently detached so as not to internalize responsibility for the child's problem? Can we respect the child's right to work through the process? Can we help without assuming the role of parent? Can we accept the fact that we can not always help as much as we wish we could?

14. Can we function for the children with unconditional acceptance? Are their feelings really okay with us? Can we remain non-judgmental?

15. Are we skilled at validating and affirming other people simply for who they are, not for what they do?

16. How is our own spiritual life? Can we see God's hand in the healing process? Are we able to pray comfortably with children?

17. Do we have the inner peace and calm to consistently encourage the children in their struggle and to engender their trust in their own ability to cope?

18. Are we comfortable with the use of gentle confrontation and behavior management techniques which preserve the integrity of the group?

19. Are we able to seek help for ourselves when we need it?

20. Are we open to new ideas and input from children, friends, professionals, etc.?

21. Do we realize the importance of our full presence for the children as a confidant and as an accepting support person? Are we too caught up in activities and materials to be there and give of ourselves?

22. Are we able to listen and resist advice-giving? Can we let the children learn to problem-solve?

23. Are we able to refer for professional counseling, etc. when the situation calls for it?

24. Can we respect the confidentiality of the group setting?

25. Are we able to confidently direct the focus of the group discussions and/or activities? Can we keep the group on the topic? Can we avert hostile remarks, scapegoating? Can we encourage group members to support, but not join others in their pain?

26. Can we focus on empathy, not pity when dealing with children in pain?

27. Are we able to be there for children on an individual basis if they require something extra outside the group?

28. Can we be flexible to the needs of the group? Are we able to listen to what *they* need?

29. Can we deal with the parents of the children if they question what we are doing in the group?

30. Do we have sufficient active listening skills? Can we reflect back to the child what was said without questioning or advising? Can we resist demonstrating shock or responding with overt emotional displays?

SPECIAL CHALLENGES: WHAT CHILDREN BRING TO THE GROUP

1. low sense of self-worth

2. depression

3. anger and hostility

4. bitterness and resentment

5. "missed" childhood

6. separation anxiety/clinginess

7. fear

8. anxiety/distress

9. manipulation

10. emotional abandonment

11. physical abandonment

12. co-dependency

13. dominance or submissiveness

14. happy-go-lucky facade—"It doesn't really bother me."

15. overt grief

16. parental care-taking concerns

17. adolescent issues

18. despair

19. interpersonal relationship problems/peer problems

20. embarrassment

21. shame

22. feeling of responsibility

23. dysfunctional family symptoms

24. repressed feelings; denial of reality; inaccessible affect

25. attribution/failure to take responsibility

26. suicidal thoughts and tendencies

27. lying/fantasizing/embellishing

28. defensiveness

PREPARATION FOR SUNRISE

1. Determine the number of sessions you will conduct. Twelve weeks is recommended, but this is flexible.

2. Set a time to begin which is convenient for those involved. The length of the sessions is usually from 45 minutes to an hour. In a school setting it is more difficult to set the time you desire. Since students will be missing classes, you might want to rotate times.

3. Facilitators for the groups should have some orientation and training so they will understand the divorce experience, the experience of children whose parents are divorced and are well acquainted with the SUNRISE material. Facilitators need to have skills which enable them to deal effectively and compassionately with children who are hurting.

4. Determine how the SUNRISE program is going to be announced. This can be done through letters to parents, the news media, or church bulletins. It is essential that parents give consent for their children to participate in the SUNRISE program.

5. Determine the age groups you will be using. The following groups could effectively work together:

K-1-2		2-3-4
3-4-5	or	5-6-7
6-7-8		8-9
HS		HS

ANNOUNCING SUNRISE

Letter to Parent(s)

Dear Parent,

On [date] we will begin a [number of weeks] week series of sessions for children ages _____ to _____ whose parents are divorced. The group will meet from [time] to _____ at [location].

The program, SUNRISE, is a peer support group, so children will be in small groups with children their own age. SUNRISE provides a safe environment for children:
1. To deal with feelings and issues relating to their parents' divorce
2. To understand that they are not responsible for the divorce
3. To realize that the marriage is over and there is nothing they can do to change this
4. To learn skills in order to more effectively deal with issues which arise
5. To develop positive self-esteem

If you wish to have your child/children participate in this program, please fill out and return the form below by [date].

Before your child comes to the SUNRISE program, it is important that you spend some time with him/her to talk about the purpose of this group. Children will be there because they have parents who are divorced. It will be a time to talk about their own experience of the divorce. In this way children will not come to the group and be surprised by its focus.

If you have any further questions, call [group leader].

Sincerely,

Please return this form by _____ to:

_____

_____

_____

Please register my child/children in SUNRISE.

Child's Name _____ Address _____

Phone _____ City _____ Zip _____

Parent Signature _____

If different from child: Address _____ Phone _____

                         City_____ Zip _____

News Media

SUNRISE, a support group for children ages _____ to _____ whose parents are separated or divorced, will be conducted in [number] sessions at [location] from [time] to_____ beginning [date]. For registration and further information call _____.